GROSS
GUIDES
TO PSYCHOLOGY
AQA (A) AS

RICHARD GROSS
JEAN-MARC LAWTON

HODDER
EDUCATION
AN HACHETTE UK COMPANY

Picture credits

The author and publishers would like to thank the following for permission to reproduce material in this book:

Figure 2.1 © romadora – Fotolia; Figure 2.2 © Richard Bowlby; Figure 2.4 © Cameron Laird / Rex Features; Figure 2.6 © Cresta Johnson – Fotolia; Figure 4.4 © gerenme/ iStockphoto.com; Figure 5.1 © Galina Barskaya – Fotolia; Figure 5.3 © Courtesy of the American Psychological Association Archives; Figure 6.4 © JEAN-CLAUDE REVY, ISM/SCIENCE PHOTO LIBRARY; Figure 6.5 © Universal History Archive/ Getty Images; Figure 6.6 © Jason Stitt – Fotolia; Figure 7.1 © Wong Hock Weng – Fotolia; Figure 7.2 © twixx – Fotolia; image of open book used throughout © blackred / iStockphoto

Every effort has been made to obtain necessary permission with reference to copyright material. The publishers apologise if inadvertently any sources remain unacknowledged and will be glad to make the necessary arrangements at the earliest opportunity.

Acknowledgements

JML would like to thank Tim Lloyd for his friendship and encouragement over so many years, peace, love and Northern Soul.

Orders: please contact Bookpoint Ltd, 130 Milton Park, Abingdon, Oxon OX14 4SB. Telephone: (44) 01235 827720. Fax: (44) 01235 400454. Lines are open from 9.00 to 5.00, Monday to Saturday, with a 24-hour message answering service. You can also order through our website www.hoddereducation.co.uk

If you have any comments to make about this, or any of our other titles, please send them to educationenquiries@hodder.co.uk

British Library Cataloguing in Publication Data
A catalogue record for this title is available from the British Library

ISBN: 9781444168068

Published 2012
Impression number   10 9 8 7 6 5 4 3 2
Year   2016, 2015, 2014, 2013

Copyright © 2012 Jean-Marc Lawton and Richard Gross

Hachette UK's policy is to use papers that are natural, renewable and recyclable products and made from wood grown in sustainable forests. The logging and manufacturing processes are expected to conform to the environmental regulations of the country of origin.

Illustrations by Barking Dog Art
Typeset by DC Graphic Design Limited, Swanley Village, Kent.
Printed in Dubai

Contents

CHAPTER 4: STRESS

CHAPTER 5: SOCIAL INFLUENCES

CHAPTER 6: PSYCHOPATHOLOGY

EXAM GUIDANCE

How to use this book

This book will help you revise for your AS exams in the AQA (A) Psychology specification. It is designed so that you can use it alongside any appropriate textbook, including Richard Gross's *Psychology: The Science of Mind and Behaviour*, and we have included page references to material in this book on appropriate spreads.

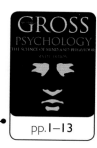

pp. 1–13

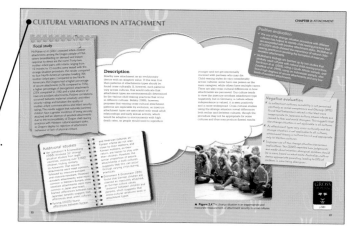

Each spread covers a different topic, outlining the headline factual knowledge you need, as well as providing evaluation material to help you aim for those top marks.

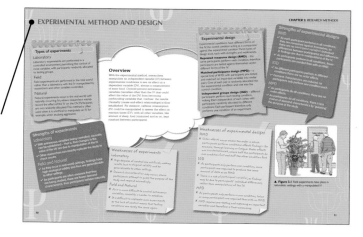

Research methods and techniques are also covered in a colourful and exciting way to help you retain and recall the information.

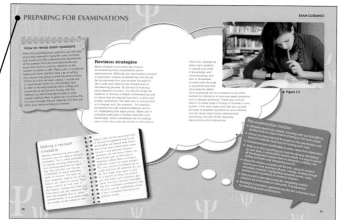

Jean-Marc Lawton is a senior examiner for a leading exam board and at the end of the book you will find his guidance on making sure you are ready to tackle the exams!

MULTI-STORE MODEL (MSM)

Focal study

Baddeley (1966) examined encoding in STM and LTM by giving 75 participants either: acoustically similar words (e.g. 'caught' 'taut'), *acoustically dissimilar* words (e.g. 'foul' 'deep'), *semantically similar* words (e.g. 'big' 'huge') or *semantically dissimilar* words (e.g. 'pen' 'ring'). With STM, acoustically dissimilar words were better recalled (80%) than acoustically similar words (10%), indicating acoustic encoding to be dominant. Semantically dissimilar words (71%) were recalled slightly better than semantically similar ones (64%), suggesting that semantic coding does occur in STM, but is not dominant.

With LTM, participants followed the same procedure, but with a 20-minute gap between presentation and recall. There was no perceivable difference between acoustically similar and dissimilar words, but more semantically dissimilar words (85%) were recalled than semantically similar ones (55%), suggesting semantic encoding is dominant in LTM.

Description

The MSM explains how data move between three permanent storage systems, each system differing in terms of:
1. **Capacity** – how much data is stored
2. **Duration** – how long data are stored
3. **Encoding** – the form in which data are stored.
Sensory memory (SM) is a limited-capacity, short-duration store containing unprocessed impressions of sensory data. Attended information goes for further processing in *short-term memory* (STM), with non-attended information not processed or immediately forgotten. SM has separate stores for sensory inputs – for example, *iconic store* for visual and *echoic store* for auditory information. STM is an active, temporary

Additional studies

- Miller (1956) reviewed literature to conclude that the capacity of STM was five to nine items, but showed how chunking could increase this by grouping information into meaningful units using established memory stores.
- Peterson & Peterson (1959) read out nonsense trigrams to participants (e.g. XPJ), then got them to count backwards from a large digit from between 3 and 18 seconds to prevent recall. 90% of trigrams were recalled after 3 seconds, but only 5% after 18 seconds, suggesting that STM duration is between 18 and 20 seconds.

- Anonkhin (1973) estimated the number of possible neuronal connections in the brain at 1 followed by 10.5 million kilometres of noughts. As nobody can use anywhere near this potential, it suggests that LTM capacity is limitless.
- Bahrick (1975) found that participants who had left school in the last 15 years recalled 90% of faces and names of schoolmates from photos, while those who had left 48 years previously recalled 80% of names and 70% of faces. This implies that LTM duration is very long-lasting.

Positive evaluation

✔ The MSM inspired interest and research, leading to later theories like the working memory model. Case studies indicate that brain damage can affect either STM or LTM abilities, which supports the idea of STM and LTM being separate memory stores.

✔ Murdock (1962) found that words at the beginning of a list that are rehearsed and thus in LTM (primacy effect) are well recalled, as are words at the end of the list, which are still in STM (recency effect). This further supports the idea of separate STM and LTM stores.

memory system, holding information in use. The dominant encoding type in STM is *acoustic*, with other sensory codes also used. Capacity is limited to five to nine items, extended by *chunking*, where the size of the units of information is increased. Duration is limited to around 30 seconds; though rehearsal retains data within the STM loop, until eventually becoming more permanent within *long-term memory* (LTM). The dominant encoding type in LTM is *semantic*, though other encoding types also occur, such as *visual* and *acoustic*. Potential capacity is assumed to be unlimited, with duration possibly lifelong. Unlike STM, information in LTM does not have to be continually rehearsed to be retained, with forgetting occurring mainly not due to loss of data, but to retrieval failures.

Negative evaluation

✘ The MSM is oversimplified as seeing STM and LTM as single stores. Research suggests several types of STM, such as separate stores for verbal and non-verbal sounds and different types of LTM, such as procedural, episodic and semantic.

✘ Cohen (1990) thinks memory capacity is not measurable necessarily by the amount of information, but by the nature of the information to be recalled. MSM does not consider this.

✘ Research indicates that rehearsal is not the only factor in the transfer of material from STM to LTM, contradicting MSM.

✘ MSM focuses too much on memory structure rather than processes.

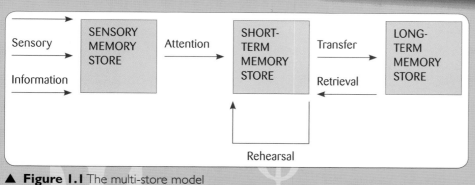

▲ **Figure 1.1** The multi-store model

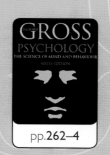

pp.262–4

WORKING MEMORY MODEL (WMM)

Focal study

Alkhalifa (2009) examined the existence of the EB, by presenting 48 students with numerical information on a screen, either in sequential fashion (e.g. 1, 2, 3, 4) or in parallel fashion, where information was presented in different parts of the screen simultaneously. Numbers were used of sufficient complexity to override the capacities of both the PL and the VSS. Participants were set problem-solving questions based on the numbers presented. Those using sequentially presented material were superior, which suggests that a limitation exists on information passing from perception to learning, as parallel processing was a hindrance to learning. As sequential processing was superior, it indicates that the capacity of WM is larger than that determined by the capacity of the PL and the VSS, implying the existence of a limited-capacity EB, which acts as a temporary 'general store' of integrated material.

Description

Replacing the single STM of the MSM, the WMM proposes a four-component working memory based on the form of processing each carries out. The limited capacity *central executive* (CE) acts as a filter, dealing with sensory information of all types, and determines what information is attended to and allocates this information to 'slave systems', temporary stores dealing with different types of sensory information.

The *phonological loop* (PL) is a slave system dealing with auditory information. It is similar to the rehearsal system of the MSM, with a limited capacity determined by the amount of information spoken in about 2 seconds. It divides into the *phonological store* (PS), which stores

Additional studies

- D'Esposito et al. (1995) found, using fMRI scans, that the pre-frontal cortex was activated when verbal and non-verbal tasks were performed simultaneously, but not when performed separately, suggesting that the brain area is associated with the CE.

- Baddeley et al. (1975) found with the PL that lists of words that took longer to pronounce were not recalled as well as lists of the same number of words pronounced more quickly, which suggests that the capacity of the PL is limited by the amount of time it takes to say them.

- Smith & Jonides (1999) found that with visual tasks PET scans showed activation in the brain's left hemisphere, but activation in the right hemisphere with spatial information, supporting the idea of the VC and the IS being separate entities.

- Baddeley & Lewis found that participants knew which nonsense words were homophones (words that sound the same, but have different meanings) even when using their PL for a different task, which suggests the PAS is separate from the PL.

Positive evaluation

✓ The idea that any one slave system, like the PL, can be involved in performing many different tasks, like memory, mental arithmetic, verbal reasoning and reading, is a valuable insight.

✓ The WMM is more plausible than the MSM, as it demonstrates STM in terms of temporary storage and active processing.

✓ Unlike the MSM, the WMM does not overemphasise the importance of rehearsal for STM retention.

✓ The WMM suggests practical applications, especially for children with learning difficulties associated with problems of impairments in working memory.

words heard, and the *articulatory process* (AP), which permits sub-vocal repetition of information stored in the PL. The *primary acoustic store* (PAS) was a later addition, which stores recently heard speech and sound. Another slave system is the *visuo-spatial sketch-pad* (VSS), a temporary store for visual and spatial items and the relationships between them. It divides into the *visual cache* (VC), which stores visual material concerning form and colour, and the *inner scribe* (IS), which stores information about spatial relationships.

A third slave system is the *episodic buffer* (EB), which integrates information from the CE, PL, VSS and LTM.

Negative evaluation

✗ WMM only deals with STM and therefore is not a comprehensive model of memory.

✗ The WMM does not explain changes in processing ability occurring as the result of practice or time.

✗ It is not clear how the CE operates, this vagueness being used to explain all findings. If two tasks cannot be performed simultaneously, it is concluded that the processing components are conflicting or that the tasks exceed CE capacity. If two tasks can be performed simultaneously, it is concluded that they do not exceed available resources.

✗ Much research into the WMM is laboratory-based and therefore lacking in mundane realism.

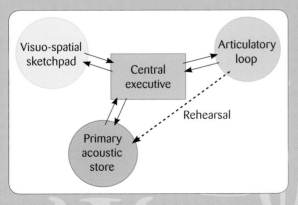

▲ **Figure 1.2** The working memory model

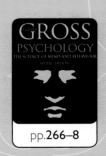

GROSS
PSYCHOLOGY
THE SCIENCE OF MIND AND BEHAVIOUR
SIXTH EDITION

pp.266–8

EYEWITNESS TESTIMONY • MISLEADING INFORMATION

Focal study

Loftus & Palmer (1974) believed EWTs were unreliable due to misleading questions. Forty-five participants watched films of car accidents and were asked 'how fast were the cars going when they _____ into each other'. The missing verb was one of smashed/bumped/collided/hit/contacted. More severe verbs like 'smashed' resulted in higher speed estimates. The mean estimates in m.p.h. were: 'smashed' 40.5, 'collided' 39.3, 'bumped' 38.1, 'hit' 34.0, 'contacted' 31.8. In a second experiment, 150 students watched a film of a car crash with no broken glass occurring. One-third were asked 'how fast were the cars travelling when they smashed into each other'; for another third 'smashed' was replaced with 'hit'; and for the final third no estimate of speed was required. A week later, 32% in the 'smashed' condition recalled broken glass, compared to 14% in the 'hit' condition and 12% in the control condition. The combined findings show that the misleading information in the verb used to describe speed affected the way information was represented in memory so that memories were reconstructed, including the new information, resulting in false memories.

Description

Eyewitness testimony (EWT)

EWT concerns the accuracy of memories from eyewitnesses. In 75% of cases where DNA shows wrongful convictions, original judgment occurred through inaccurate EWT. Bartlett (1932) explained how memories are not accurate 'snapshots' of events, but reconstructions influenced by schemas, ready-made expectations based on previous experiences, moods, existing knowledge, contexts, attitudes and stereotypes. Therefore eyewitnesses do not passively recall events as they happen, but reconstruct memories biased by active schemas at time of recall. In court, some barristers are accused of 'leading witnesses', posing questions that affect schemas and suggest certain answers, not necessarily accurate ones.

Additional studies

- Loftus & Pickrell (2003) found that more childhood visitors to Disneyland, given fake Disneyland adverts featuring Bugs Bunny (not a Disney character) and with a cardboard Bugs Bunny in the room, recalled meeting Bugs Bunny compared to those who read adverts with no cartoon characters and without the cardboard figure present. This suggests that misleading information creates false memories.
- Brigham & Malpass (1985) found that errors in identification were likelier to happen when witnesses and suspects are racially different, which suggests that race can affect accuracy of EWT.

- Bekerian & Bowers (1983) showed slides of events leading up to a car crash, finding that participants' memories were unaffected by misleading questions, which suggests that post-event information affects retrieval of memories rather than their storage.
- Loftus (1975) found that 17% of witnesses to a film of a car journey featuring no barn, recalled one when asked a week later 'how fast was the car going when it passed the white barn?' supporting the notion of post-event information affecting EWT.

Positive evaluation

✔ Memory for important aspects of events is not easily distorted by misleading information, only unimportant aspects, possibly due to the amount of attention allocated to different aspects.

✔ Research into EWT suggests practical applications in the ways court cases are conducted and how witnesses are interviewed. Guilty verdicts are now unadvisable via uncorroborated EWT alone.

✔ Loftus's work has increased understanding of the area and stimulated research to identify important factors involved in EWT, like age and anxiety.

Misleading information

Research shows that EWT is affected by experiences occurring after witnessed events, a prime factor being the use of misleading information, especially from misleading questions. These take two forms: (1) *leading questions* – questions increasing the chances that people's schemas influence them to recall incorrect answers; and (2) *post-event information* – misleading information added to questions after incidents occur, negatively affecting later recall.

Negative evaluation

✘ It is unclear with misleading information whether errors in recall occur due to demand characteristics or actual changes in the memory of events.

✘ Laboratory studies are artificial. Foster et al. (1994) showed that EWT was more accurate for real-life crimes than simulated ones, probably because the consequences of inaccurate recall are greater with real-life incidents and participants are more emotionally involved.

✘ Home Office advice to juries about EWT is based on judicial intuition (common-sense analysis) rather than any systematic review of research evidence, which suggests that errors and therefore wrongful convictions may still occur.

✘ Inaccurate recall in experiments is expected, as participants do not expect to be misled.

▲ Figure 1.3

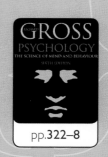

GROSS
PSYCHOLOGY
THE SCIENCE OF MIND AND BEHAVIOUR
SIXTH EDITION

pp.322–8

EFFECTS OF ANXIETY ON MEMORY

Focal study

Yuille & Cutshall (1986) investigated the effects of arousal on recall of an armed robbery where a thief stole guns and money, but was shot six times by the shopkeeper outside the shop and died, the shopkeeper being seriously wounded too. The police interviewed all 21 witnesses, and five months later the researchers re-interviewed 13 of these, aged between 15 and 32 years. Two misleading questions were inserted by the researchers during the re-interview. Eyewitness accounts to the police and researchers were analysed. Accuracy of recall was very high, especially among the most aroused participants, and the misleading questions had no effect. These results contradict laboratory studies, where misleading questions did create inaccurate recall; indeed the results suggest that heightened arousal is associated with accurate memory, though the most stressed were also closer to the crime and therefore had the best view.

Description

Anxiety is associated with witnessing real-life crimes/incidents, as they often have a high emotional impact and can draw attention away from the important aspects of a situation. Some research suggests that anxiety can lessen an individual's field of vision, meaning that some possibly important aspects are not encoded into memory, while other research implies that arousal can actually improve the accuracy and detail of recall. Deffenbacher (1983) used the *inverted-U hypothesis* to explain this, by arguing that moderate levels of emotional arousal improve recall up to an optimal point of arousal, after which any additional increases in emotional arousal lead to a gradual decrease in recall quality. Such data plotted on a graph forms an inverted (upside-down) 'U' shape.

Additional studies

- Loftus et al. (1987) found that participants focused more on a weapon a person was carrying than on their face, which suggests that facial details of armed criminals would not be recalled, supporting the idea that anxiety diverts attention from important details of incidents.
- Ginet & Verkampt (2007) found that participants with moderate anxiety recalled more details of a traffic accident viewed on film than those with low arousal, suggesting that increased arousal benefits recall, in line with the inverted-U hypothesis, although high arousal was not assessed.
- Oue et al. (2001) found that participants anxious from watching emotionally negative events recalled fewer details from the periphery of a scene than non-anxious participants who viewed emotionally neutral events, supporting the idea that anxiety reduces the field of view.
- Koehler (2002) found that participants recalled non-stressful words better than stressful ones, supporting Freud's concept of repression, though Hadley & McKay (2006) found better recall of stressful words, as they were memorable, suggesting that repression occurs only in some instances.

▼ **Figure 1.4** The inverted-U hypothesis

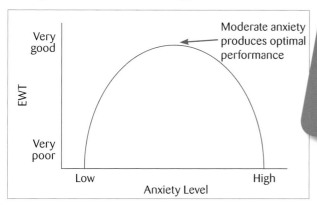

Freud offers an alternative explanation by the means of *repression*, where anxiety hampers the recall of traumatic events, because such memories are hidden (repressed) in the unconscious mind in order to protect individuals from their emotionally distressing nature. Such memories are accessible by psychotherapy, where therapists help individuals by various techniques to recover such 'hidden' memories, but have led to accusations of *false memory syndrome*, where incorrect memories occur due to being 'suggested' to individuals by their therapists. Such retrieval of memories is currently banned.

Negative evaluation

✗ In 2004 Deffenbacher reviewed his results, finding them oversimplistic. From a meta-analysis of 63 studies he found that EWT performance increased gradually as arousal rose, in line with the inverted-U hypothesis, but with very high levels of anxiety, recall did not decline gradually, but decreased with a catastrophic drop in accuracy.

✗ Laboratory studies of anxiety and recall accuracy are inferior as there is not the personal emotional involvement found with real-life incidents, and witnesses may be more aware of the importance of memorising details fully and accurately for later recall in possible legal proceedings.

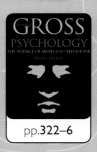

GROSS
PSYCHOLOGY
THE SCIENCE OF MIND AND BEHAVIOUR
SIXTH EDITION

pp.322–6

▲ **Figure 1.5**

EFFECTS OF AGE ON MEMORY

Focal study

Coxon & Valentine (1997) tested age differences in susceptibility to misleading information. 52 children, 53 young adults and 42 elderly people with a mean age of 70 years watched a video of a kidnapping and then answered questions, which for half the participants in each group contained four misleading questions – for instance, 'Which arm did the kidnapper have her watch on?' when there was no watch. Young adults were superior to children and the elderly in accuracy of recall, measured by how many questions they got right, but the elderly proved less suggestible to misleading questions than the young adults. It was concluded that young children and the elderly are less accurate and therefore make less reliable eyewitnesses, but also that the recall of different age groups is qualitatively different, with elderly people remembering less, but having more reliable memories. This also goes against the idea of the elderly being more prone to misleading information.

Description

Research indicates that memory ability declines with age, but this is not a unanimous view; indeed research findings from all age groups are not consistent, possibly due to methodological faults, and several factors have been identified that moderate the effect of age on accuracy of recall. Children also make less accurate witnesses, again with several factors involved. Older people tend to have less accurate and less detailed recall of events than young people and the middle-aged, and tend to be more prone to being misled by leading information. There is

Additional studies

- Memon & Thomson (2007) found 60- to 80-year-old adults likelier to choose incorrect faces from a selection of photos compared to 18- to 32-year-olds, which implies that reduced perceptual abilities and visual acuity, as well as difficulties in storing and retrieving information, affect EWT.

- Hammond & Thole (2008) found that children make less effective witnesses, as their memories are less efficient and they are less articulate. This implies a problem with children's ability to communicate memories, which has implications for how they are questioned.

- Robert & Lamb (1999) found that in interviews with children who were making accusations of abuse, investigators misinterpreted or distorted children's reports, but these inaccuracies went unchallenged by children, which suggests that children accept inaccuracies for fear of contradicting adults.

- Loftus et al. (1991) found the elderly likelier to make false identifications, poorer at recalling specific details and that elderly men were affected by misleading post-event information, which suggests that accuracy of recall declines with age and that there is increased vulnerability to misleading information.

✔ Research suggests practical applications in the way child eyewitnesses are questioned, as they are especially vulnerable to inaccuracies in recall due to misleading questions. There are special procedures in place in courts of law and with police interviews in terms of the ways in which children are questioned.

✔ Research has also helped to reduce age-based stereotypes about memory, with individual differences in memory ability being recognised in all age groups, especially the elderly, and also the recognition that there are qualitative differences in recall between age groups, rather than just overall memory ability differences.

also a reported tendency for the elderly to make false identifications and to have poorer recall of specific details. Children are likelier to accept false information supplied by adults, because of a fear of contradicting adults, but generally have more accurate and detailed recall when they identify an event as serious. Research also suggests that the accuracy of children's recall is very dependent on how they are questioned. Younger children seem especially at risk of being misled by leading questions and post-event information, and this has serious implications for how children are interviewed by police officers and in courts of law.

Negative evaluation

✘ It is unclear why age differences exist. The superior performance of young adults may be due to being more motivated and more used to tests, while poor physical health may explain why some elderly people have poor memory ability.

✘ Many studies use samples of elderly people from care homes who have reduced memory ability anyway and therefore do not form representative samples.

✘ One methodological consideration is that college students are often compared with the elderly, but on tests and stimuli more suited to college students, which may negatively affect results.

▲ **Figure 1.6** How reliable are the eyewitness testimonies of elderly people?

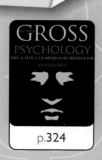

GROSS
PSYCHOLOGY
THE SCIENCE OF MIND AND BEHAVIOUR
SIXTH EDITION

p.324

THE COGNITIVE INTERVIEW (CI)

Focal study

Geiselman *et al.* (1985) showed a police training film of a violent crime, with participants interviewed 48 hours later using either the standard interview technique, or hypnosis and the standard interview technique, or the new CI. The amount of false information produced by all three techniques was the same, but the standard interview produced the least overall amount of information and the CI the most, an average of 41.2 items compared to 29.4 items. A second experiment then introduced misleading information during the interview – for instance, '*Was the guy with the green backpack nervous?*' (It wasn't green.) Participants tested with the CI were least likely to be misled. These results strongly suggest the CI to be a superior form of police interview than the standard technique in the amount of accurate material recalled and the lower amount of false information recalled in response to misleading information.

Description

The cognitive interview replaced the standard police interview, which depended on free recall of events, and is an interview procedure facilitating accurate, detailed recall, based on Tulving's (1974) idea that several retrieval paths to memory exist and if one path is not accessible, another one may well be. The CI also makes use of Tulving & Thomson's *encoding specificity theory* (1973), which suggests the use of as many retrieval cues as possible to improve recall.

The CI has four components:

1. *Change of narrative order* – where events are recalled in different chronological orders – for example, from end to beginning.

2. *Change of perspective* – where events are recalled from different perspectives – for example, from the offender's point of view.

Additional studies

- Bekerian & Dennett (1993) reviewed 27 studies, comparing the effects of the CI with standard techniques, finding the CI better in all cases. On average around 30% more information is accurately recalled, with false information less common, supporting the idea of the CI being a superior technique.

- Geiselman & Fisher (1997) found that the CI works best when used within a short time following a crime rather than a long time afterwards, suggesting some limitations in its usage.

- Milne & Bull (2002) found the 'report everything' and 'context reinstatement' components of the CI to be the key techniques in gaining accurate, detailed recall, which implies that some components of the CI are more effective than others.

- Ginet & Py (2001) found that usage of the CI resulted in a significant increase in the amount of accurate material recalled by eyewitnesses without a comparable increase in the number of errors produced, suggesting the CI to be effective.

Positive evaluation

✔ Fisher & Geiselman (1988) have continued to develop the CI using information gained from watching 'good' and 'poor' interviewers. This has led to more open-ended questions and fitting the order of questioning to the witness's order of experience, increasing accuracy of recall from 40% to 60%.

✔ Harrower (1998) maintains that the CI procedure is especially beneficial in the interviewing of child witnesses, particularly when physical and/or sexual abuse is involved. However, such interviewers must be trained in assessing the linguistic and cognitive competence of each child interviewee and adapt the interview accordingly, illustrating the need for skilled, trained interviewers.

3. *Mental reinstatement of context* – which makes use of environmental context – for example, weather and emotional context (feelings) of the crime scene.

4. *Report everything* – where all information is recalled, even that which seems trivial or muddled.

Fisher *et al.* (1987) produced the *enhanced cognitive interview* (ECI) to overcome problems caused by inappropriate sequencing of questions. Extra features include (a) *minimisation of distraction*; (b) *reduction of anxiety*; (c) *getting witnesses to speak slowly*; (d) *asking open-ended questions*.

Negative evaluation

✘ Although an effective technique, the CI is prone to false positives, where incorrect information is recalled.

✘ The CI can be time-consuming, often taking longer than police officers have operational time for.

✘ The CI comprises several techniques and, as different police forces use different versions, comparisons are difficult.

✘ The CI is only recommended for witnesses aged 8 years and above, as younger witnesses produce less accurate information than with other interview techniques.

✘ 'The change of perspective' component can mislead witnesses into speculating, so is less frequently used.

▲ **Figure 1.7**

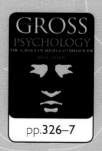

GROSS
PSYCHOLOGY
THE SCIENCE OF MIND AND BEHAVIOUR
SIXTH EDITION

pp.326–7

STRATEGIES FOR MEMORY IMPROVEMENT

Description

There are several techniques to improve recall. *Retrieval cues* act as triggers to prompt memories and occur as two types:

1. *External (context-dependent) cues* where being in the same physical environment as where material was encoded facilitates recall.

2. *Internal (state-dependent) cues* where being in the same internal physiological state as when encoding material facilitates recall.

Chunking involves increasing the capacity of STM by grouping individual bits of information into larger 'chunks' by giving them a collective meaning to make them comprehensible. For example, reading involves chunking letters into words and words into sentences.

Additional studies

- Abernethy (1940) used familiar/unfamiliar tutors and teaching rooms to find that participants tested by familiar tutors in familiar rooms had better recall, suggesting that external retrieval cues are a useful strategy for memory improvement.
- Baddeley et al. (1975) found that chunking was affected by the *word length effect*, which concerns the length of words being chunked, with better recall of short rather than long words. This suggests that smaller chunks are more effective in facilitating recall.
- Baltes & Kliegl (1992) found that older adults should use verbal mnemonics, as they found it hard to produce and recall visual images necessary for visual imagery mnemonics. This suggests that the ability to use different types of mnemonics changes over one's lifespan.
- Morris (1985) found that football fans recall scores better than non-fans as they process them – for example, by comparing scores to expected scores. This suggests that active processing is a useful strategy for memory improvement.

A third method is *mnemonics*, where recall is facilitated by organising material, such as imposing a structure on material to be recalled. *Visual imagery mnemonics* focus on visual images, like the rooms of a house, with items to be recalled placed in the rooms and visualised. *Verbal mnemonics* focuses on words, usually by using acronyms where information to be recalled is formed from the first letters of other words – for example, '**E**very **G**ood **B**oy **D**eserves **F**un' forms **EGBDF**, which are musical notes. Finally, *active processing* refers to procedures where learners go beyond passive, unthinking encoding of information, instead subjecting material to deep, meaningful processing.

Positive evaluation

✔ Chunking is effective for students, as they periodically have to learn and recall vast amounts of information.

✔ Practical use is made of internal and external retrieval cues by ensuring that revision and examinations take place in circumstances as similar as possible to when material was learned.

✔ Visual imagery mnemonics are most effective in learning and recalling actual objects rather than abstract concepts and ideas.

✔ Active processing is a dynamic theory, perceiving memory as a process, not a set of passive stores. It therefore provides meaningful links between memory and other cognitive areas.

Negative evaluation

✗ Much research supporting retrieval cues is laboratory-based and unlike everyday memory. For example, performing procedural memory tasks, like riding a bike, is unaffected by retrieval cues.

✗ Small chunks with fewer amounts of items are recalled better than large chunks with greater amounts of items, suggesting some limitations to chunking.

✗ The ability to use visual imagery mnemonics depends on how much individuals are 'high imagers' or 'low imagers', suggesting that it is not effective for everyone.

✗ Active processing is a circular concept that is untestable and unscientific. Strongly processed material is recalled better, but better recalled material must also have been actively processed.

ITVABCSOSFBILOLTNT

SOS

ITV

LOL

FBI

ABC

TNT

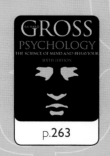

p.263

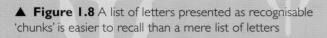

▲ **Figure 1.8** A list of letters presented as recognisable 'chunks' is easier to recall than a mere list of letters

LEARNING THEORY

Focal study

Harlow (1959) tested learning theory by comparison of attachment behaviour in infant monkeys. Condition one consisted of a cage containing a wire mother producing milk and a towelling mother producing no milk. Condition two consisted of a cage containing a wire mother producing no milk and a towelling mother producing milk. Condition three consisted of a cage containing a wire mother producing milk. Condition four consisted of a cage containing a towelling mother producing milk. Time spent feeding and with each surrogate mother was recorded. A loud noise tested for mother preference during stress. The infants preferred the towelling mother regardless of whether she produced milk and clung to her when stressed. Monkeys with only a wire surrogate had diarrhoea, a sign of stress. It was concluded that monkeys have an innate need for contact comfort, which suggests that attachment concerns emotional security more than food. This therefore is evidence against learning theory.

Description

Learning theory sees all behaviour as learned by experience and association. *Classical conditioning* occurs when stimuli become associated with innate responses; therefore attachments form when infants learn to associate their caregivers with food, an *unconditioned* or *primary reinforcer*, due to the pleasure that eating food brings. This association between an infant and the sense of pleasure forms the attachment bond. Caregivers are *conditioned* or *secondary reinforcers*, as they satisfy their infants' biological need for nutrition, which explains why the theory is also known as *cupboard love* theory. Caregivers eventually become reinforcing in their own right, as infants will feel secure with their presence

Additional studies

- Schaffer & Emerson (1964) studied 60 infants at 4-weekly intervals throughout their first year and again at 18 months, finding that infants also formed attachments to people not performing caregiving, usually fathers. In 39% of cases the primary attachment figure was not the main caregiver who fed the infant, usually the mother. This goes against the learning theory of attachment.

- Dollard & Miller (1950) calculated that in their first year, infants are fed 2,000 times, giving ample opportunity for the caregiver, as a form of negative reinforcement, to become associated with removal of hunger. This supports the idea of attachment occurring through operant conditioning.

- Fox (1977) studied attachment relationships in mothers, infants and *metapelets* on Israeli kibbutzim (communal farms). Metapelets provide the majority of care for infants while mothers work. Generally, infants were more attached to their mothers, some showing little if any attachment to their metapelets. As metapelets do most of the feeding, this goes against learning theory.

Positive evaluation

✓ Although ultimately a theory that was not supported by research and therefore refuted as an explanation of attachment behaviour, learning theory did stimulate a lot of interest in the area, leading to subsequent better explanations, which created a greater understanding of the behaviour.

✓ Learning theory comes from the behaviourist tradition, a very scientific form of psychology that lends itself to rigorous scientific analysis and objective measurement. Therefore the theory, as all scientific theories should, permitted itself to be refuted, so that alternative explanations could be formulated and tested.

without the need for feeding.

Another aspect of learning theory is *operant conditioning*, where behaviour is learned due to its consequences via the use of reinforcements, which increase the chances of behaviour occurring again. Therefore attachments occur via operant conditioning, through infants' caregivers becoming associated with reducing unpleasant feelings of hunger, thus becoming a source of reinforcement themselves. In this instance, food is a *primary reinforcer*, as it directly reinforces attachment behaviour by reducing hunger. Caregivers are *secondary reinforcers*, as they become associated with supplying the food that reduces the hunger.

Negative evaluation

✗ Schaffer (1971) argued that the learning theory puts things the wrong way round; babies do not 'live to eat', but 'eat to live', and thus are active seekers of stimulation, not passive recipients of nutrition.

✗ Although conditioning via feeding plays some part in attachment behaviour, food does not appear to be the main explanation of the behaviour.

✗ Conditioning explains the acquisition of simple behaviours, but not more complex behaviours like attachment, which has an intense emotional component.

✗ Bowlby (1973) argues that babies only periodically need food, but continually require the emotional security that attachment provides, again casting doubt on learning theory.

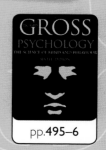

GROSS
PSYCHOLOGY
THE SCIENCE OF MIND AND BEHAVIOUR

pp.495–6

▲ **Figure 2.1** Learning theory sees feeding as the key to attachment formation

BOWLBY'S THEORY

Focal study

Lorenz (1935) had a duckling as a small boy and noticed its close bond with him. Lorenz later tested this by splitting a clutch of greylag geese eggs into two groups. One group hatched normally to be raised by the mother, the goslings following her around from birth. The second clutch was artificially incubated so that Lorenz was the first thing seen on hatching. Instantly they followed him, having created an 'imprint' of Lorenz to follow. Lorenz then put the whole clutch together under an upturned box, having first marked 'his' goslings. On release the goslings went to their respective mother figures, the first group to the mother goose and the second group, showing no recognition of their mother, to Lorenz. In adulthood the goslings attempted to mate with Lorenz. The findings suggest that imprinting is an innate, irreversible attachment behaviour that bestows an adaptive advantage.

Description

Bowlby was influenced by Lorenz's work on *imprinting*, an innate behaviour where newborn birds follow the first moving object encountered within a *critical period*. Bowlby saw attachment as an evolutionary device, where emotional bonds develop to help protect infants from predators. Attachment behaviour is genetically programmed and is naturally selected for its survival value. *Social releasers*, innate species-specific behaviours, facilitate the attachment process. These include *crying* to attract a caregiver's attention, *looking/smiling/vocalising* to maintain the caregiver's attention and *following/clinging behaviour* to gain and maintain physical closeness to caregivers. Attachment behaviours become increasingly focused only on caregivers, with adults genetically programmed to respond

Additional studies

- Rutter (1981) found that infants display a whole range of attachment behaviours towards a variety of attachment figures other than mothers; indeed there is no particular attachment behaviour used specifically and exclusively for mothers. Therefore mothers are not special in the way Bowlby claimed.

- Schaffer & Emerson (1964) followed 60 infants at 4-weekly intervals for their first year and then again at 18 months, finding multiple attachments the norm, with 87% of children forming more than one attachment and 33% five or more by 18 months of age, which goes against Bowlby's notion of monotropy, where infants display a prime attachment to just one figure.

- Lamb (1982) studied the relationships infants formed with fathers, grandparents, siblings and so on, finding that different attachments served different purposes, with infants tending, for example, to go to fathers for play and mothers for comfort, going against Bowlby's monotropic idea of attachment being a hierarchy, with mother at the top.

Positive evaluation

✔ There is a lot of evidence to support some aspects of Bowlby's theory – for example, the **continuity hypothesis**, which predicts a consistency between early emotional experiences and later adult relationships.

✔ Bowlby's theory puts attachment behaviour into an evolutionary perspective, which explains its existence and development as having occurred via natural selection. Infants who exhibited such behaviour had an adaptive advantage and thus survived to sexual maturity, furthering their genes that precipitated attachment behaviour, with the behaviour eventually becoming commonplace in the population.

sensitively to infants' signals. Bowlby sees attachment as a control system maintaining a steady state whereby infants remain close to caregivers. If the steady state is threatened by caregivers' absence or the presence of strangers, attachment behaviours are used to regain the steady state. Babies are seen as *monotropic*, having an innate tendency to attach to the person who interacts with them most sensitively, usually the mother, with attachments needing to form before three years of age or they will not form at all. Attachments also form an *internal working model*, a template for later adult relationships.

Negative evaluation

✗ Imprinting applies mainly to precocial species that are mobile soon after birth and therefore may not apply to humans.

✗ Bowlby sees attachments forming due to mere exposure of infants to caregivers. However, Schaffer & Emerson's (1964) study showed that attachments form with adults displaying the most sensitive responsiveness, where they identify and respond appropriately to an infant's needs. This suggests that attachment formation is a more dynamic process than Bowlby claimed.

✗ Bowlby did not see a role for fathers in his theory, seeing them as not of direct emotional importance to an infant's upbringing. However, research suggests that attachments to fathers are of importance, such as in their provision of stimulating play.

▲ **Figure 2.2** John Bowlby

GROSS
PSYCHOLOGY
THE SCIENCE OF MIND AND BEHAVIOUR
SIXTH EDITION

pp.496–7

THE STRANGE SITUATION AND TYPES OF ATTACHMENT

Focal study

Ainsworth et al. (1978) tested 106 young infants between 9 and 18 months old under conditions of mild stress and novelty, to assess *stranger anxiety, separation anxiety* and the *secure base concept*. The strange situation procedure involved an 81-square-foot new environment divided into 16 squares to track movements and consisted of 8 episodes involving mothers and strangers in various scenarios of arrival and departure. Five categories were recorded: *proximity and contact-seeking behaviours, contact-maintaining behaviours, proximity and interaction-avoiding behaviours, contact and interaction-resisting behaviours* and *search behaviours*. Every five seconds the category of behaviour was recorded and assessed on a scale of 1–7. 15% of infants were *insecure-avoidant* attachment type, 15% were *insecure-resistant* and 70% were *securely attached*. Ainsworth concluded that *sensitive responsiveness* was the key factor, as sensitive caregivers are accepting, co-operative and accessible, attending appropriately to their infant's needs. Sensitive mothers tend to have securely attached infants.

Description

Ainsworth, a student of Bowlby's, devised the *strange situation* procedure, which became the paradigm (accepted) method of identifying and measuring attachment types. She observed and interviewed 26 Ugandan mothers, with infants ranging from 15 weeks to 2 years of age, from which she identified three attachment types:

1. *Securely attached* (Type B), where children are willing to explore, have high stranger anxiety, are easy to soothe and are enthusiastic at their caregiver's return. Caregivers are sensitive to their infants' needs.

2. *Insecure-avoidant* (Type A), where children are willing to explore, have low stranger anxiety, are indifferent to separation and avoid contact at the return of their caregiver. Caregivers ignore their infants.

Additional studies

- Main & Solomon (1986) reported another attachment type, *insecure-disorganised* (Type D), exhibited by a few infants, whose behaviour is a confusing mix of approach and avoidant behaviours.

- Vaughn et al. (1980) found that attachment types changed according to variations in family circumstances, especially changes of accommodation and mothers' stress levels, suggesting that attachment types are not permanent characteristics.

- Main et al. (1985) found that 100% of infants securely attached before 18 months were still securely attached at age 6, with 75% who were anxious-avoidant remaining so. As children tested at different times generally retained attachment types, it suggests the strange situation is reliable, producing consistent results over time.

- Main & Weston (1981) found that infants displayed different attachment types depending on which parent they were with. For instance, an infant might be classed as insecure-avoidant with their mother, but securely attached with their father, suggesting the strange situation measures not attachment types, but the quality of relationships between individuals.

Positive evaluation

✔ The strange situation is accepted as the established (paradigm) methodology for assessing attachment behaviour.

✔ Van Ijzendoorn & Schuengel (1999) see Ainsworth's studies as important, as her central finding of parental sensitivity being linked to the quality of attachment has been widely replicated by others using larger samples.

✔ Although the strange situation attracts criticism for being unethical, as it subjects infants to stress, it is modelled on everyday experiences where mothers do leave children for brief periods in different settings and with strangers – for example, babysitters.

3. *Insecure-resistant* (Type C), where children are unwilling to explore, have high stranger anxiety, are distressed at separation, and seek and reject contact at the return of caregivers. Caregivers show simultaneous opposite feelings and behaviour towards their infants.

Ainsworth believes that there are two distinct features of attachment, both with adaptive survival value. First, infants seek proximity to the caregivers, especially when threatened, and second, secure attachments permit infants to explore, essential for social and cognitive development, using the attachment as a safe base from which to explore and return to.

Negative evaluation

✗ Rutter et al. (2009) believe that the strange situation focuses too much attention on the secure/insecure aspects of attachment and neglects other important aspects of the behaviour.

✗ It may be incorrect to assume that insecure attachments are maladaptive, as from an evolutionary perspective, differing environmental conditions would mean that there would be circumstances where insecure attachment types would be adaptive.

✗ The strange situation is an artificial way of assessing attachment, being laboratory-based and with mothers and strangers acting to a script. Brofenbrenner (1979) found that infants' attachment behaviour is stronger in a laboratory than at home.

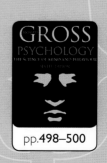

GROSS
PSYCHOLOGY
THE SCIENCE OF MIND AND BEHAVIOUR
SIXTH EDITION

pp.498–500

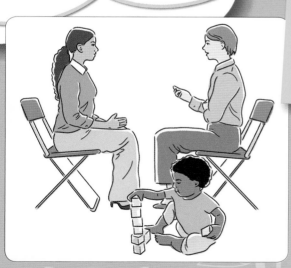

▲ **Figure 2.3** Episode 3 of the strange situation

CULTURAL VARIATIONS IN ATTACHMENT

Focal study

McMahan et al. (2001) assessed infant–mother attachments among the Dogon people of Mali, where breastfeeding on demand and instant response to stress are the norm. Forty-two mother–infant pairs, with infants ranging from 10 months to 12 months, were tested with the strange situation procedure, the results compared to four North American samples totalling 306 mother–infant pairs. Compared to the North Americans, the Dogons had a higher percentage of secure attachments (67% compared to 55%), a higher percentage of disorganised attachments (25% compared to 15%) and a total absence of insecure-avoidant attachments. Positive correlations occurred between maternal sensitivity and infant security ratings and between the quality of mother–infant communications and infant security ratings. The results suggest that naturally parented children have a greater incidence of being securely attached and an absence of avoidant attachments due to the incompatibility of Dogon child-rearing practices with Western cultural avoidant styles, as Dogons display no rejection of attachment behaviour or lack of physical contact.

Description

Bowlby saw attachment as an evolutionary device with an adaptive value. If this was true then patterns of attachments types should be found cross-culturally. If, however, such patterns vary across cultures, this would indicate that attachment types are environmentally determined by the various child-rearing practices that occur in different cultures. Belsky (1999), however, proposes that varying cross-cultural attachment patterns are explicable by evolution, as insecure attachment types are associated with weak adult relationships and early sexual activity, which would be adaptive in environments with high death rates, as people would need to reproduce

Additional studies

- Van Ijzendoorn & Kroonenberg (1988) reviewed 32 strange situation studies from eight countries, involving over 2,000 children, finding, similarly to Ainsworth, that secure attachments were most common, followed by insecure-avoidant and insecure-resistant. However, avoidant attachments were more common in Western Europe, while resistant attachments were more common in Japan and Israel. Marked differences between two Japanese samples suggest that differences exist within cultures.
- Kyoung (2005) found differences between Korean and American cultures, as Korean infants do not stay close to their mothers, and Korean mothers, on their return, are likelier to play with their children. However, the similar proportion of secure attachments in both cultures suggests that this can occur through varying child-rearing practices.
- Grossmann & Grossmann (1991) found that German children are classed as insecurely attached, as German culture values 'distance' between children and parents, which suggests that cross-cultural variations exist in attachment types.

Positive evaluation

✔ The use of the strange situation procedure with different cultures has helped to identify child-rearing practices that are associated with positive attachment styles. McMahan et al.'s (2001) study showed the importance of natural child-rearing practices in avoiding the formation of insecure-avoidant attachments.

✔ McMahan's findings are backed up by two studies that similarly used cultures with natural child-rearing practices; Tomlinson et al. (2005), using a South African sample, and Zevalkink et al. (1999), using an Indonesian sample, also found high degrees of secure attachments and very low levels of avoidant attachments.

younger and not get emotionally involved with partners who may die. Child-rearing styles do vary considerably across cultures; some have one person as the main caregiver, while others have multiple carers. There are also cross-cultural differences in how attachments are perceived. Our culture tends to view the insecure-avoidant attachment type negatively, but in Germany, a culture where independence is valued, it is seen positively and is more widespread. Cross-cultural studies using the strange situation reveal differences both *within* and *between* cultures, though the procedure may not be appropriate for some cultures and thus may produce flawed results.

Negative evaluation

✗ In collectivist cultures, sociability is not perceived positively as social competence and Okonogi (1992) found that behaviours valued in the West were inappropriate to Japanese culture, where infants are reared to fear and avoid strangers. This suggests that the strange situation is not applicable in all cultures.

✗ As attachment types vary cross-culturally and the strange situation is not applicable to all cultures, attachment theory is culture-bound and appropriate only to Western cultures.

✗ Improper use of the strange situation has serious implications. Yeo (2003) reported how judgements are made about whether aboriginal children should be in care, based on what white Australian culture deems appropriate parenting, leading to 25% of children in care being aborigines.

▲ **Figure 2.4** The strange situation is an inappropriate and inaccurate measurement of attachment security in some cultures

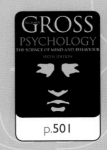

GROSS
PSYCHOLOGY
THE SCIENCE OF MIND AND BEHAVIOUR
SIXTH EDITION

p.501

THE DISRUPTION OF ATTACHMENT

Description

Bowlby's *maternal deprivation hypothesis* (1951) states that disruption of attachment leads to serious, irreversible social, emotional and intellectual damage. Attachments are disrupted in two ways, each with different developmental impacts: first, *deprivation*, either short-term like being in day care, or long-term, like family break-ups, and second, *privation*, where attachments never formed. The effects of short-term separation are:

1. *Protest*, where children express anger and fear by screaming, kicking and so on.

2. *Despair*, where anger and fear are inwardly experienced, but exterior protest is replaced by apathetic, calmer behaviour.

Additional studies

- Freud & Dann (1951) reported on six orphans, aged 3 to 4 years, rescued from a Nazi concentration camp. They had little language, refused to be separated and displayed hostility to adults. They gradually formed attachments with their carers, making rapid physical and intellectual development. Follow-up studies suggested that their recovery was full and permanent.

- Quinton & Rutter (1976) reported that behavioural problems were more common in adolescents who had been separated from attachment figures in the first five years of life, demonstrating the long-term effects of short-term separations.

- Hetherington & Stanley-Hagan (1999) found that 25% of children had long-term adjustment problems after parental divorce, but most eventually adapted, which suggests that the effects of long-term separation are reversible.

- Schaffer (1996) found that nearly all children are negatively affected by divorce in the short term, which suggests that the effects of long-term deprivation are universal.

Positive evaluation

✔ Findings from studies of privation suggest that recovery is possible if subsequent loving relationships are experienced.

✔ The close attachments the Czech twins and the Holocaust children had with each other may explain why they recovered. In other cases, individuals without such relationships did not recover.

✔ Case studies are used, as other research methods would be unethical.

✔ Research into short-term separation through hospitalisation led to radical changes in hospital practices, with nurses' shifts designed so that they had regular contact with the same children, giving opportunities for alternative attachments to form.

3. *Detachment*, where everyone is treated warily and caregivers rejected on their return. The effects of long-term separation are more pronounced, with children being negatively affected in social development, emotional well-being, self-concept, academic performance and physical health. Evidence suggests that these effects are not necessarily long-term.

Privation is researched through case studies and studies of institutional care, which suggest that the effects of privation are more damaging and can lead to *affectionless psychopathy*, where a personality lacking in social conscience forms, creating problems in establishing intimate, two-way emotional relationships.

Negative evaluation

✗ Case studies depend on retrospective memories that may be inaccurate or incomplete. There is no way of truly knowing what happened to individuals before discovery.

✗ Bowlby's perception of attachment disruption leading to serious, permanent damage seems overstated. There are several examples of full recovery from severe deprivation and privation.

✗ Individual differences have not been considered. Securely attached children cope well with separations, suggesting that it is only some children who are negatively affected.

✗ Most evidence linking short-term separation to negative outcomes is correlational and does not show causality. Other factors may also play a role.

✗ The effects of long-term separation are not universal: disruption through divorce leads to stress and resentment, while disruption through death of an attachment figure leads to depression and delinquency.

▲ **Figure 2.5** Short-term separations are characterised by protest, distress and despair

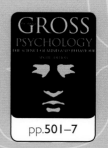

GROSS PSYCHOLOGY
THE SCIENCE OF MIND AND BEHAVIOUR

pp.501–7

THE EFFECTS OF DAY CARE ON AGGRESSION AND PEER RELATIONS

Focal study

Borge et al. (2004) assessed whether day care was associated with increased physical aggression in children. Data from a maternal questionnaire on 3,431 Canadian 2- to 4-year-olds compared physical aggression rates between children raised at home and children attending day care. A family risk index examined occupational status, maternal education, number of siblings and the degree of family functioning, to determine the contribution of family features to aggression levels. Aggression was more prevalent in children raised at home. Assessment then concentrated on whether higher levels of aggression occurred within identifiable sub-groups. After taking family features into consideration, which were related to aggression levels, it was revealed that physical aggression was more common in children of high-risk families raised at home. These families had low levels of maternal education, three or more siblings, low socio-economic status and poor family functioning. It was concluded that home care is associated with higher aggression levels in pre-school children, especially those from high-risk families.

Description

Day care refers to temporary non-maternal care of children living with their families – for example, nurseries, kindergartens. The care of children outside of family homes raises passionate arguments, some seeing it as harmful to development, while others believe it to be beneficial. It is difficult to get an unbiased, objective outlook, as many opinions are biased by philosophical/political viewpoints – for instance, those who see a woman's place at home raising children. However, the reality is, through economic necessity, most parents work. In 2004 52% of women with children under 5 years of age worked. Therefore research focuses on what comprises good day care practices, so they can

Additional studies

- Clarke-Stewart et al. (1994) found that children with superior abilities in negotiating with peers were those who attended day care, implying that day care is effective in creating good peer relationships.
- Gunnar et al. (1997) found that socially incompetent children had negative peer interactions, suggesting that day care is harmful to some children.
- Hartup & Moore (1990) found that day care allows children to interact more extensively with peers and thus to learn social interaction skills, suggesting that day care helps to develop positive peer relations.
- Egeland & Heister (1995) found that insecurely attached children progressed well with day care, but securely attached children reacted aggressively to the extra attention, suggesting that day care is harmful to some children.
- Doherty (1996) reported less aggression in children attending day care, but only with low staff–children ratios, trained staff and stimulating environments, suggesting that high-quality care helps to maintain low aggression levels.
- Durkin (1995) found that pre-schoolers attending day care from early infancy were more prone to aggression, suggesting that the age children begin day care is important.

Positive evaluation

✓ Research mainly indicates that day care provides most children with increased chances for social contact and the development of social skills that create positive peer relations.

✓ Good-quality day care is not related to the amount of day care received, but to quality. Sensitive day care applicable to individual children's needs is more crucial than the amount of time carers spend with children.

✓ Children from disadvantaged backgrounds benefit most in reducing aggressiveness from attending day care; this suggests that day care has a compensatory effect on aggression levels in such children.

be adopted, and what comprises poor day care practices, so they can be eradicated. Research has focused especially on the effects of day care on aggression and peer relations, with emphasis on assessing whether day care is harmful for certain age groups, whether there are individual differences between children in how day care affects them, and what constitutes good day care. Research suggests that certain types of children experience heightened aggression and poor peer relations through day care and that factors exist that contribute to negative developments in these areas.

Negative evaluation

✗ Research often confuses aggression with rough-and-tumble play and therefore evidence of heightened aggression may be a misreading of non-aggressive behaviour.

✗ Day care is an area contaminated with bias. Belsky (2009) argues that policymakers should stop selectively embracing data that are consistent with their biased, pre-existing viewpoints and dismissing data that are not.

✗ Aggressive children are likelier to be placed in day care to give their parents a break, which suggests that day care itself may not be responsible for elevated aggressiveness.

✗ Day care may harm the development of peer relations, especially for those who are socially incompetent; indeed day care presents opportunities for them to be identified and bullied.

▲ **Figure 2.6**

THE INFLUENCE OF ATTACHMENT AND DAY CARE RESEARCH ON CHILDCARE PRACTICES

Focal study

Belsky & Rovine (1988) examined the effect of babies placed in day care at a young age due to mothers having to return to work, something that was becoming increasingly common. Data from two longitudinal studies of infants and family development were combined and subjected to analysis. A total of 149 infants comprised the sample, aged between 12 and 13 months, 90 of whom were male and 59 female. The sample contained children from both working-class and middle-class backgrounds and only contained children from married parents. 43% of infants who attended day care for at least 4 months before their first birthday and for more than 20 hours a week were more likely to be classified as insecurely attached to the mother and to avoid the mother on reunion than were infants in care fewer than 20 hours per week (26%). The results suggest that young children attending day care for lengthy periods are vulnerable to having attachments negatively affected.

Description

Originally, day care, due to the influence of Bowlby's maternal deprivation hypothesis, was perceived as incurring irreversible, harmful consequences. However, research has indicated that high-quality day care benefits children, and attention has been concentrated on identifying factors advantageous to developmental outcomes. Current thinking is that very young children should not attend day care for lengthy periods, as it negatively impacts on attachments and social development. Day care also seems to affect children differently, insecurely attached children being negatively affected in social development, leading to suggestions that children entering day care should be assessed, so that those

Additional studies

- Andersson (1989) assessed Swedish children on cognitive and social competence, finding that children entering day care early performed better cognitively and in social-personal development than children entering day care later and children reared at home. This contradicts Belsky & Rovine (1988), which suggests that the high quality of Swedish day care contributed to the positive outcomes.

- Rout et al. (1997) found working mothers superior to non-working mothers on levels of mental health, which suggests that day care benefits mothers too in their ability to interact positively with their children.

- NICHD (1997) found that insecurely attached children attending day care had poor social development. This suggests that certain types of children are vulnerable to negative outcomes from day care, which was backed up Pennebaker et al. (1981), finding that shy children did not incur positive social development with day care.

- Holloway & Reichart-Erickson (1988) found that children engaging in high-quality interactions, with low child–staff ratios and stimulating materials performed well cognitively, which suggests that positive development is linked to high-quality care.

vulnerable to negative effects could be specially catered for. Research also suggests that child-minding could be a positive and effective means of childcare if childminders received similar training to those providing high-quality day care. Mothers benefit from day care too, as it frees them from the stresses of childcare and heightens self-esteem by being able to work, thus making them more effective mothers who interact more positively with their children. The characteristics of high-quality day care are identified as:

- *verbal interaction between carers and children*
- *provision of stimulating activities*
- *sensitive emotional care*
- *low staff turnover, consistency of care*
- *mixed age groups*
- *structured, timetabled activities.*

▲ **Figure 2.7** Groups comprising mixed ages allow younger children to learn social behaviours through observation and imitation

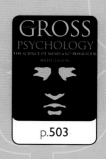

GROSS
PSYCHOLOGY
THE SCIENCE OF MIND AND BEHAVIOUR
SIXTH EDITION

p.503

EXPERIMENTAL METHOD AND DESIGN

Types of experiments

Laboratory

Laboratory experiments are performed in a controlled environment, permitting the control of most variables, with participants randomly allocated to testing groups.

Field

Field experiments are performed in the 'real world' rather than a laboratory, with the IV manipulated by researchers and other variables controlled.

Natural

Natural experiments occur in the real world with naturally occurring IVs, where researchers merely record the effect of the IV on the DV. Participants are not randomly allocated. This method is often used when it is unethical to manipulate an IV for example, when studying aggression.

Overview

With the experimental method, researchers manipulate an *independent variable* (IV) between experimental conditions to see its effect on a *dependent variable* (DV), always a measurement of some kind. *Controls* prevent *extraneous variables* (variables other than the IV that could affect the value of the DV) from becoming *confounding variables* that 'confuse' the results. *Causality* (cause-and-effect relationships) is thus established. For instance, caffeine consumption (IV) could be manipulated to assess the effect on reaction times (DV), with all other variables, like amount of sleep, food consumed and so on, kept constant between participants.

Strengths of experiments

Laboratory

✓ With extraneous variables being controlled, causality can be established – that is, that changes in the value of the DV are due to manipulation of the IV.

✓ Other researchers can exactly replicate the study to check results.

Field and Natural

✓ As they occur in real-world settings, findings have high ecological validity and thus are generalisable to other settings.

✓ As participants are often unaware that they are being studied, there are fewer demand characteristics, thus participants behave naturally.

Weaknesses of experiments

Laboratory

✗ High degrees of control are artificial, making results lack ecological validity and be generalisable to other settings.

✗ Demand characteristics may occur, where participants attempt to guess the purpose of the study and respond accordingly.

Field and Natural

✗ As it is more difficult to control extraneous variables, causality is harder to establish.

✗ It is difficult to replicate such experiments, as the lack of control means that testing conditions are rarely the same again.

Experimental design

Experimental conditions have different forms of the IV, the *control condition* acting as a comparison against the *experimental condition*. Three types of design exist, each with strengths and weaknesses.

Repeated measures design (RMD) – the same participants perform each condition, therefore participants are tested against themselves under different forms of the IV.

Matched participants design (MPD) – a special kind of RMD, with participants pre-tested and matched on important variables into similar pairs. One of each pair is randomly allocated into the experimental condition and one into the control condition.

Independent groups design (IGD) – different participants perform each testing condition, making them independent of each other, with participants randomly allocated to different conditions. Each participant therefore only performs one condition of an experiment.

Strengths of experimental designs

RMD

✔ As each participant performs in all conditions, they are compared against themselves, so there are no **participant variables** (individual differences between participants) and differences in findings are due to manipulations of the IV.

✔ As participants perform in all conditions, fewer participants are needed than with an RMD.

IGD

✔ As different participants perform in different conditions there are no order effects.

✔ Demand characteristics are reduced, as participants only perform one condition each.

MPD

✔ As participants do all conditions, there are no order effects.

✔ As participants do all conditions, there is less chance of demand characteristics by 'guessing' the purpose of the study.

Weaknesses of experimental designs

RMD

✘ Order effects occur where the order in which participants perform conditions affects findings— for example, through learning or fatigue. Order effects are counterbalanced, where half the participants do one condition first and half the other condition first.

IGD

✘ As participants only perform one condition, more participants are required to produce the same amount of data as an RMD.

✘ There is a risk of participant variables, as findings may be due to participants' individual differences, rather than manipulations of the IV.

MPD

✘ As participants only perform in one condition, twice as many participants are required than with an RMD.

✘ MPD requires pre-testing and matching on important variables and therefore is time-consuming.

▲ **Figure 3.1** Field experiments take place in naturalistic settings with a manipulated IV

NON-EXPERIMENTAL METHODS AND DESIGN

Correlational analysis

Correlational analysis involves assessing the degree of relationship between two or more co-variables – for example, between the number of hours of sleep and the score on a memory test. A *positive correlation* occurs when one co-variable increases as another co-variable increases – for example, sales of umbrellas increase as the number of days it rains increases. A *negative correlation* occurs when one co-variable decreases while another increases – for example, sales of bikinis decrease as the number of days it rains increases. A *correlational co-efficient* is a numerical value expressing the degree to which co-variables are related. Measurements range between +1.0, a perfect positive correlation, and −1.0, a perfect negative correlation.

Strengths

- Correlations do not require manipulation and are used when experiments would be unethical.
- Once correlations are established, predictions can be made, like how many umbrellas will be sold on rainy days.

Weaknesses

- Correlations are not conducted under controlled conditions and therefore do not show causality.
- Apparently low correlations can actually be statistically significant if the number of scores used is sufficiently high.

Overview

Non-experimental (*alternative*) research methods differ from experiments in that they do not have an IV or a DV, are not conducted under controlled conditions and are therefore difficult to replicate, and do not show causality (cause-and-effect relationships). Each has strengths and weaknesses and is more appropriate to different types of research aims.

Observations

Observations generally involve measuring naturally occurring behaviour in the real world. *Participant* observations involve researchers being actively involved in the behaviour being assessed. *Non-participant* observations involve researchers not being actively involved in the behaviour being assessed. *Overt* observations involve the participants knowing they are being observed, while in *covert* observations they do not.

Strengths

- Observations have high *external validity*, as they involve natural behaviour in a real-life setting, so can be generalised to other settings.
- As participants are usually unaware of being observed, there are few *demand characteristics*.

Weaknesses

- It can be difficult to remain unobserved and make accurate, full observations.
- As observations are not conducted under controlled conditions, they are difficult to replicate to check the reliability and validity of findings.

▲ **Figure 3.2** Case studies involve in-depth, detailed investigations of one person or a small group

Case studies

Case studies involve detailed, in-depth investigation of one person or a small group, usually involving biographical details, behaviour and experiences of interest.

Strengths

- Case studies allow 'difficult' areas to be investigated where other methods would be unethical, such as sexual abuse.
- Data relate specifically to one person, not an average produced from many people.

Weaknesses

- Findings only relate to one person and cannot be generalised to others.
- Case studies are usually reliant on full and accurate memories, which can often be selective and affected by researcher bias.

Self-reports

Self-reports involve participants detailing information about themselves without researcher intervention.

Questionnaires

Questionnaires are a self-report method where participants give answers to pre-set written questions, usually involving opinions, attitudes, beliefs and behaviour. **Closed** questions involve limited responses set by researchers, such as yes/no tick boxes. Answers are easy to quantify, but restricted. **Open** questions allow participants to answer fully in their own words and thus give greater depth and freedom of expression, but are less easy to quantify and analyse.

Strengths:
- Large samples can be generated by posting out questionnaires, which also means that researchers do not have to be present when they are completed.
- Questionnaires obtain lots of data relatively quickly.

Weaknesses:
- There is a possibility of idealised and socially desirable answers, with participants answering how they think they should, rather than giving honest answers.
- Questionnaires, especially those with closed questions, are not suitable for sensitive issues requiring careful and detailed understanding.

Interviews

Interviews involve asking participants face-to-face questions. **Structured** interviews involve asking identical, simple, quantitative questions to all participants, while **unstructured** interviews involve an informal discussion on set topics producing mainly qualitative data. **Semi-structured** interviews involve a mixture of structured and unstructured questions.

Strengths:
- Both quantitative and qualitative data are produced that offer a greater variety and depth of findings.
- With unstructured and semi-structured interviews, follow-up questions can be asked to explore interesting answers.

Weaknesses:
- Interviewers can bias responses through their appearance, age, gender and so on.
- Some participants may not have the verbal skills to fully express themselves.

AIMS ● HYPOTHESES ● OPERATIONALISATION OF VARIABLES ● DEMAND CHARACTERISTICS ● PILOT STUDIES

Aims

Aims are research objectives, exact statements of why studies are conducted — for instance, to investigate whether differing amounts of sleep affect concentration levels. Aims should incorporate what is being studied and what studies are trying to achieve.

Hypotheses

Hypotheses are more objectively precise than aims and are testable predictions of what is expected to happen. There are two types of hypotheses:

1. The *experimental* hypothesis predicts that differences in the DV will be outside the boundaries of chance (known as *significant differences*), as a result of manipulation of the IV. The term 'experimental hypothesis' is used with experiments; other research methods refer to 'alternative hypotheses'. For example, 'that participants receiving eight hours' sleep last night will perform significantly better on a test of concentration than those receiving four hours' sleep last night'.

2. The *null* hypothesis predicts that the IV will not affect the DV and that any differences found will not be outside the boundaries of chance – that is, will not be significantly different. For example, 'that participants receiving eight hours' sleep last night will not perform significantly better on a test of concentration than those receiving four

Operationalisation of variables

Operationalisation concerns objectively defining variables in an easily understandable manner, so that an *independent variable* (IV) can be manipulated (altered between testing conditions) and its effect on a *dependent variable* (DV) measured. For example, if researching the effect of sleep on concentration, the IV could be operationalised as the amount of sleep the previous night and the DV the score on a test of concentration. Without accurate operationalisation, results may be unreliable and invalid; therefore it is crucial to operationalise IVs and DVs accurately, but this can be difficult – for example, how can 'anger' be accurately operationalised?

Demand characteristics

Research involves social interactions between investigators and participants, which can influence and bias findings so that they are not valid. One such research effect is demand characteristics, where participants form impressions of the research purpose and unknowingly alter behaviour accordingly. Demand characteristics affect research findings in several ways:

1. Where participants guess the purpose of research and try to please researchers by giving them their expected results.

2. Where participants guess the purpose of research and try to sabotage it by giving non-expected results.

3. Where participants, out of nervousness or fear of evaluation, act unnaturally.

4. Where participants respond to a *social desirability bias* and give answers/exhibit behaviour that shows them in a socially acceptable manner.

Demand characteristics are reduced by the *single blind procedure*, where participants are not aware of which testing condition they are in – for example, in a drug trial not knowing if they have swallowed a real pill or a placebo.

hours' sleep last night. Any differences found will be due to chance factors'. One of these two hypotheses will be supported by the findings and accepted, while the other will be rejected. There are two types of experimental/alternative hypotheses:

1. *Directional* (*one-tailed*) hypotheses predict the direction that the results will lie in. For instance, 'that participants running 400 metres on an athletics track while being watched by an audience of their peers will run in significantly quicker times than those running without an audience'.

2. *Non-directional* (*two-tailed*) hypotheses predict a difference in the results, but not the direction the results will lie in. For instance, 'that there will be a significant difference in times achieved between participants running 400 metres on an athletics track while being watched by an audience of their peers and those running without an audience'.

Directional hypotheses are used when previous research gives an indication of which way findings will lie.

Pilot studies

Pilot studies are small-scale 'practice' investigations allowing procedural improvements and removal of methodological errors. Participants can point out flaws, like the presence of demand characteristics. Pilot studies show what kind of results are expected and if there is any possibility of significant results. Pilot studies permit the quality of research to be improved and help avoid unnecessary time and effort being wasted – for example, by performing lengthy studies only to find that due to unexpected errors and problems, the results are invalid and the study will have to be altered and repeated.

ETHICAL ISSUES • SAMPLING TECHNIQUES • RELIABILITY AND VALIDITY

Sampling techniques

A sample is a part of a population and should be as representative as possible – that is, possess the same characteristics as the population from which it is drawn. Several sampling techniques exist:

1. *Random sampling* occurs where all members of a population have an equal chance of being selected. Computer-generated random number lists can be used. The selection is unbiased, but samples can still be unrepresentative – for example, all females.

2. *Opportunity sampling* involves using whoever is available. Such samples are easy to obtain, but often unrepresentative – for example, all students.

3. *Self-selected sampling* involves using volunteers, usually responding to advertisements. It involves minimal effort to obtain participants, but often provides biased samples, as volunteers can be a certain 'type' of person and so eager to please that demand characteristics occur.

Ethical issues

To protect the dignity and safety of participants, as well as the integrity of psychology, research should be conducted in an ethical manner. Full details of research should be submitted to the appropriate ethical committee for approval before commencing. The British Psychology Society publishes a code of ethics that researchers should follow:

1. *Informed consent* – participants should be fully informed of the objectives and details of research to make a considered decision about whether to participate. Parental consent is obtained for under 16s.

2. *Deception* – misleading of participants and withholding information should be avoided.

3. *Protection of participants* – participants should not be put at risk of harm and should leave a study in the same state they entered it.

4. *Right to withdraw* – participants should be aware that they can leave at any time, including withdrawing their data in the future.

5. *Confidentiality* – participants' data should not be disclosed to anyone, unless agreed in advance.

Reliability

If findings are reliable, they are consistent. If a study were repeated exactly, the same results should be obtained. There are two ways to assess reliability.

1. Internal reliability concerns whether findings are consistent within themselves – for example, a measurement of height should measure the same distance between 2 metres and 4 metres, as between 5 metres and 7 metres.

2. External reliability concerns whether findings are consistent over time – for example, an IQ test should produce the same level of intelligence for an individual on different occasions, as long as their level of intelligence remains the same. This form of assessment is known as the *test–re-test* method.

Validity

If findings are valid they accurately measure what they claim to measure. Findings can be reliable, but not valid – for example, if the sum 2+2 is totalled three times and each time the answer is 5, the answer is reliable, but not valid. There are two ways to assess validity.

1. **Internal validity** concerns whether findings are due to the manipulation of the IV or confounding variables. To be internally valid, studies must have no researcher effects, no demand characteristics, use standardised instructions and random samples.

2. **External validity** concerns whether findings can be generalised to a wider population and to different settings and times.

6. *Anonymity* – participants are referred to by numbers, not names, so that data cannot be traced back to them.

7. *Inducements to take part* – participants should not be encouraged to participate through offers of financial gain or other gratification.

8. *Observational research* – observations should only occur in environments where people would expect to be observed.

9. *Cost–benefit analysis* – only if the benefits of research, in terms of knowledge gained and so on, outweigh the costs, in terms of possible harm to participants and so on, should the research be undertaken.

If deception is unavoidable there are measures that can be taken:

1. *Presumptive consent* – people of a similar nature are given full details of a study and asked if they would have been willing to participate. If so, it is assumed that the real participants would not object.

2. *Prior general consent* – participants agree to be deceived, but without knowing how it will occur.

3. *Debriefing* – immediately a study finishes, participants should be given full details and the right to withdraw their data. This applies to all studies, not just those involving deception, and also helps to alleviate possible psychological harm, so that participants leave in the same state they entered.

▲ **Figure 3.3** To be ethical, research must not harm participants

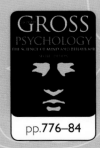

pp.776–84

37

PRESENTATION OF QUANTITATIVE DATA

Overview
Quantitative data occur as numbers, which, when presented through graphs and tables, give viewers an easily understandable visual interpretation.

Tables

Raw data are not presented in tables; instead an appropriate summary of the data is shown, such as totals, means and ranges. Individual scores are not presented, as they are displayed in the raw. As with graphs, tables should be clearly labelled and titled.

Table 3.1 Example of a table

The average number of aggressive acts a week in children attending different hours of day care	
Number of hours' day care a week	Average number of aggressive acts per week
0–5	1
5–10	3
10–15	2
15–20	4
20–25	2
25–30	3
30–35	9

Graphs

Graphs should be fully and clearly labelled on both the x and y axes and be appropriately titled, with presentation occurring best if the y-axis is three-quarters of the x-axis width. Only one graph should be used to display a set of data. Inappropriate scales should not be used, as these convey misleading, biased impressions. Different types of graphs exist for different forms of data. *Bar charts* display data as comparable categories – for example, findings from young and old participants. The columns of the bars should be the same width and separated by spaces to show that the variable on the x-axis (horizontal) is not continuous. Data are 'discrete', occurring, for example, as the mean scores of several groups. Percentages, totals and ratios can also be displayed. *Histograms* display continuous data, such as test scores, and these are displayed as they increase in value along the x-axis, without spaces between them to show their continuity. The frequency of the data is presented on the y-axis (vertical). The column width for each value

Measures of central tendency
- Measures of central tendency display the 'mid-point' values of sets of data.
- The **mean** is calculated by totalling scores and dividing by the number of scores. Its strengths are that it is the most accurate measure of central tendency and includes all scores. Its weaknesses are that it is skewed by extreme scores and may not actually be one of the scores.
- The **median** is the central value of scores in rank order. With an odd number of scores, this is the middle number, while with an even number of scores, it is the average of the two middle scores. Its strengths are that it is not affected by extreme scores and is easier to calculate than the mean. Its weaknesses are that it lacks the sensitivity of the mean and can be unrepresentative in a small set of data.
- The **mode** is the most common value. Its strengths are that it is less affected by extreme scores and, unlike the mean, is always a whole number. Its weaknesses are that there can be more than one mode and it does not use all scores.

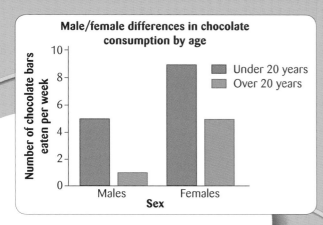

▲ **Figure 3.4** An example of a bar chart

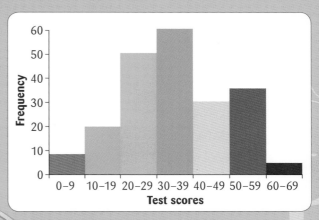

▲ **Figure 3.5** An example of a histogram

on the x-axis is the same width per equal category interval, so that the area of each column is proportional to the number of cases it represents on the histogram. *Frequency polygons* (line graphs) are similar to histograms in that the data presented on the x-axis are continuous. A frequency polygon is constructed by drawing a line from the mid-point top of each column in a histogram to allow two or more frequency distributions to be displayed on the same graph, thus allowing them to be directly compared with each other.

Measures of dispersion

1. Measures of dispersion are measures of variability in a set of data.

2. The range is calculated by subtracting the lowest from the highest value. Its strengths are that it is easy to calculate and includes extreme values, while its weaknesses are that it is distorted by extreme scores and does not indicate if data are clustered or spread evenly around the mean.

3. The interquartile range displays the variability of the middle 50% of a set of data. Its strengths are that it is easy to calculate and is not affected by extreme scores, while its weaknesses are that it does not include all scores and is inaccurate if there are big intervals between scores.

4. Standard deviation measures the variability of a set of scores from the mean. Its strengths are that it is more sensitive than the range, as all values are included, and it allows the interpretation of individual values, while its weaknesses are that it is more complex to calculate and is less meaningful if data are not normally distributed.

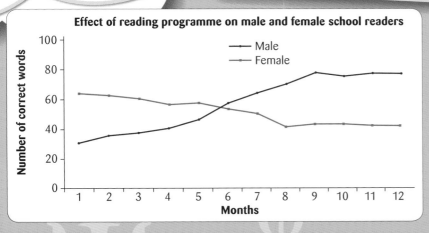

▲ **Figure 3.6** An example of a frequency polygon

PRESENTATION OF CORRELATIONAL AND QUALITATIVE DATA

Qualitative data

Qualitative data convey rich information about human experience that is lost when data merely occur in numerical quantitative form. Qualitative data generally concern experiences, descriptions and meanings, usually in the form of verbal, written and pictorial representations, and are often utilised when researching into attitudes, beliefs and opinions. There is no 'best type' of qualitative data, and as it is a fairly new area of analysis, new forms are constantly emerging and evolving, especially with the advent of new forms of technology, such as computers and interactive phones. Several forms of qualitative data currently exist.

Correlational data

Correlational studies assess the degree of relationship between co-variables, the data produced forming either positive or negative correlations (and, very rarely, no correlation). A perfect positive correlation is expressed as $+1.0$, while a perfect negative correlation is expressed as -1.0, with smaller correlations declining up or down towards zero. Correlational data are presented on a type of graph known as a *scattergram* (scattergraph) that displays the extent to which two co-variables are related, though a statistical test has to be performed to calculate the exact *correlation co-efficient* (degree of relationship).

Content analysis

Content analysis is an analytical method generally used with media research and involves the quantification of qualitative material (the transformation of qualitative data into quantitative data so that it can be numerically analysed). This can involve the assessment of speech, drawings, advertisements, newspapers and so on – for example, the analysis of what men and women are looking for in partners through analysis of 'lonely hearts' advertisements in newspapers, by scoring the amount of times certain qualities are offered or sought, like 'resources' and 'attractiveness'. Content analysis therefore requires the development of *coding units* that are used to sort material to be categorised, such as the number of times women and men appear in photographs in newspaper sports supplements. Content analysis performed in this manner can involve spoken and written words, themes, characters, time and space and so on.

Categorising

Categorising involves the grouping together of common items in discrete categories. For example, it would be possible to group different types of food items into categories that reflected their degree of healthiness, such as their fat content and energy value. The establishment of criteria that determine the categories to be used and their separateness from each other is crucial to any meaningful analysis being performed.

Quotations

The use of exact 'word-for-word' quotations can supplement research findings to highlight essential qualities in an easily understandable manner, giving them extra rich detail and bringing them to life. The selection of which actual quotations to use is essential to the realisation of this aim.

Qualitative data

... and naturalistic observations

During observational studies, researchers often record running commentaries into a tape recorder. These data are then categorised or coded into discrete categories, helping to add rich detail to quantitative data. The *diary method* is another technique used in observational studies, where observers record notes on behaviour in a self-reported manner. The diary method provides genuine information in the participants' own environments, although there are problems with this being maintained over long periods.

... and questionnaires

With self-reports, data are generally collected from open-ended questions where respondents produce answers in their own words. Data like this are less likely to be biased by interviewers' preconceived viewpoints. Analysis of such data tends to involve content analysis, categorisation and the use of quotations.

... and interviews

Because interviews are usually transcribed (converted from spoken to written form), they can be analysed by the various qualitative techniques already mentioned, like content analysis, categorisation and the use of quotations. Unstructured interviews are best for qualitative analysis, though interpretation of data from interviews is prone to biased interpretation. The lack of objectivity is more than compensated for by the level of detail created.

Evaluation of qualitative data analysis

Qualitative data can be subjective, though reliability and validity can be assessed. Researchers who favour qualitative data believe the subjectivity and personal opinions contained within qualitative data strengthens research studies, though qualitative data analysis can be time-consuming.

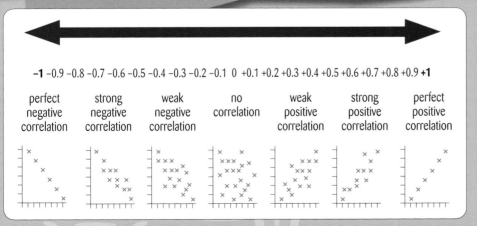

▲ **Figure 3.7** Scattergrams and correlation strength

THE PITUITARY-ADRENAL SYSTEM (PAS) AND THE SYMPATHO-MEDULLARY PATHWAY (SMP)

Focal study

Horwatt *et al.* (1988) assessed the effects of stress on the SMP by subjecting rats to the same stressor, being placed in water, each day for several weeks, finding that several adaptive changes occurred in the SMP, including the increased production and storage of *catecholamines*, flight or fight hormones that are produced in response to stress. When these animals were then subjected to a new stressful stimulus, they displayed an exaggerated response of the SMP compared to animals that were exposed to the same stressful situation for the first time, but who had not experienced the original stressor. The conclusion reached was that acute stress responses develop differently, due to previous stress experiences.

Description

The SMP comprises the *sympathetic nervous system* (SNS) and the *sympathetic adrenal medullary system* (SAM). Acute (short-lasting) stressors activate the two divisions of the *autonomic nervous system* (ANS):

1. The SNS, which acts as a 'troubleshooter' by responding to stimuli and being responsible, when activated, for emotional states and elevated arousal.

2. The *parasympathetic nervous system* (PSNS), which acts as 'the housekeeper' by maintaining equilibrium and reducing bodily processes. The two divisions of the ANS interact to produce an individual's bodily state, with the sympathetic division being the component primarily activated by stressors.

Additional studies

- Taylor *et al.* (2000) found that acute stressors produce a 'flight or fight response' in males, but a 'tend and befriend' response in females, arguably because females produce more oxytocin, a chemical that promotes relaxation and nurturing, suggesting a gender difference in the workings of the SMP.

- McCarty (1981) found that older and younger rats had equal blood plasma levels of stress hormones, before being subjected to stress, but that older rats had lower levels after being stressed, which implies that the SMP has diminished responsiveness with age.

- Watson *et al.* (2004) found elevated cortisol levels in bipolar depressives, including those in remission, suggesting that PAS maladaptiveness is involved in the disease process underpinning bipolar depression.

- Heim *et al.* (2000) found elevated PAS responses to stress in females who had endured sexual abuse in childhood, suggesting that PAS hypersensitivity, due to CRF hypersecretion, results from childhood abuse, but that CRF-receptor antagonist drugs could be used to treat conditions related to such early-life stress.

On exposure to acute stressors, the SNS becomes activated, while simultaneously the SAM system stimulates production of the hormone adrenaline into the bloodstream from the adrenal glands in the adrenal medulla, preparing the body for 'fight or flight' by increasing available oxygen and glucose to the brain and muscles, while suppressing non-emergency processes, like digestion.

The PAS is activated by chronic (prolonged) stress, prompting the *hypothalamus*, in the brain, to stimulate production of *corticotrophin-releasing factor* (CRF) into the bloodstream. This activates the pituitary gland to produce *adrenocorticototropic hormone* (ACTH) into the bloodstream, which goes to the adrenal glands, stimulating the production of stress-related hormones, like *cortisol*, allowing a steady supply of energy via blood sugar that permits individuals to deal with stressors. Cortisol helps greater pain toleration, but also leads to diminished cognitive ability and immune system performance.

Negative evaluation
✗ A lot of research into stress systems involves the use of animals, but presents a problem of extrapolation, because the stress responses of animals do not necessarily correspond to those of humans. For instance, humans are considered to have more of a cognitive element to their stress responses than animals.
✗ Research findings often cannot be generalised to females, as they were excluded from experiments on the basis that monthly fluctuations in female hormone levels would produce stress responses that varied too considerably to generate useful, valid data.

▲ **Figure 4.1** The SMP deals with acute, short-term stressors

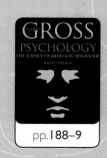

GROSS
PSYCHOLOGY
THE SCIENCE OF MIND AND BEHAVIOUR
SIXTH EDITION

pp.188–9

STRESS AND THE IMMUNE SYSTEM

Focal study

Kiecolt-Glaser (1984) assessed immune system functioning in response to stressful events. 49 male and 26 female volunteer first-year medical students gave blood samples one month before sitting their final exams and then again on the first day of their exams, after sitting two exam papers. Blood samples were analysed for leucocyte activity, specifically *killer cell* activity, which is known to fight off viruses and cancerous cells. Questionnaires were also completed to assess psychiatric conditions, loneliness and life events. Killer cell activity was found to be greatly reduced in the second blood samples compared to the first blood samples. Immune activity was also found to be lowest in participants who scored highly for loneliness, stressful life events and psychiatric conditions, such as depression and anxiety. Therefore it was concluded that stress is particularly associated with immunosuppression, especially in those individuals who are exposed to certain types of stressor.

Description

The immune system is a collection of billions of cells made mainly in the spleen, lymph nodes, thymus and bone marrow, which travel through the bloodstream, moving in and out of tissues and organs to defend the body against *antigens* (foreign agents), such as bacteria, viruses and cancerous cells, with the major type of cells being *leucocytes* (white blood cells). Some immune cells produce *antibodies*, which bind to antigens and destroy them. The study of psychological effects on the immune system is known as *psychoneuroimmunology*. When stressed, the body's ability to resist antigens is weakened, increasing vulnerability to infection. Stress does not cause infection, but instead increases the

Additional studies

- Sternberg (2000) found that when the immune system is activated to fight illness it sends signals to the hypothalamus to produce stress hormones and these shut off the immune response. This negative feedback loop therefore prevents the immune system from getting carried away and thus a little stress is healthy, but chronic stress produces such a constant flow of cortisol that the immune system is dampened too much, leading to illness.
- Kiecolt-Glaser (1995) found that the healing process in women given small wounds took longer in those who cared for senile relatives, suggesting that prolonged, chronic stress weakens immune system functioning.
- Cohen (1993) found that participants were likelier to develop a cold after being subjected to the virus if they had high-stress scores, suggesting that stress leads to immunosuppression.
- Evans (1994) found that students giving mildly stressful public presentations displayed heightened levels of sigA, an antibody that strengthens the immune system's capacity to fight infection, suggesting that short-term stress is biologically beneficial.

Positive evaluation

✔ A practical application of research into stress and the immune system is that health practitioners can use knowledge gained to help anticipate problems that occur as a response to stressful situations, like post-operative stress, and use appropriate treatments.

✔ Although prolonged, chronic stress can lead to immunosuppression and infection, short-term acute stress can be enjoyable, like watching horror films, and can actually strengthen the immune system and thus incur greater protection against immunosuppression and illness.

body's susceptibility to infectious agents by *immunosuppression*, the temporary reduction of immune functioning. Stress is associated with certain infectious diseases, like influenza, herpes and chronic fatigue disorder. Occasional release of cortisol and other corticosteroids does not damage the immune system, but if they are continually produced, as with chronic, prolonged stress, they begin to impair leucocyte activity and the production of antibodies. Therefore cortisol and so on helps protect against viruses and heal damaged tissues, but too much suppresses the immune system's ability to protect the body.

Negative evaluation

✘ Sternberg & Gold (1997) warn that immune system responses 'are so powerful that they require constant regulation to ensure they are neither excessive nor indiscriminate and yet remain effective. When the immune system escapes regulation, autoimmune and inflammatory diseases or immune deficiency syndromes result.'

✘ Research investigating the immune system and stress is only correlational and cannot show cause-and-effect relationships. Other factors may be involved, like smoking.

✘ Changes in immune system functioning as a response to stress can take time to occur and are not immediately identifiable by research. Longitudinal studies could help to show the functioning of the immune system, in response to stress, over extended periods.

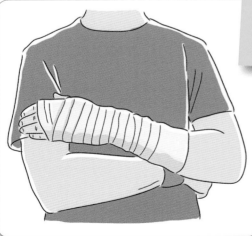

▲ **Figure 4.2** Stress lowers immune system functioning so that wounds take longer to heal

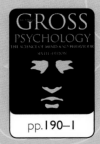

GROSS PSYCHOLOGY
pp.190–1

LIFE CHANGES AND DAILY HASSLES

Focal study

Holmes & Rahe (1967) investigated the effect of life change stressors, after Holmes noticed he developed a cold every time his mother-in-law came to stay. They examined 5,000 patients' medical records, making a list of 43 life events, of varying seriousness, which clustered in the months preceding illness. A hundred judges were told 'marriage' had a score of 500 and they then gave values to the other life events. From this, the SRRS was developed, which measures the amount of stress experienced in a given time, as *life change units* (LCUs). Only six events were seen as more stressful than marriage, like death of a spouse. Individuals with high LCU scores for the last year were vulnerable to developing stress-related illnesses in the next year, a score of over 300 LCUs being classed as a major crisis, incurring an 80% risk of illnesses like heart attacks, leukaemia and sports injuries.

Description

Much research into stress looks at the effects of everyday stressors, such as big life changes like getting married, as well as daily hassles like commuting to work. Life changes are occasional events incurring big adjustments to lifestyle, although there is a lot of variation in the effects such events have on individuals. Divorce may be traumatic for many, but for some it may bring a welcome relief from abusive relationships. The non-occurrence of desired life changes can also be stressful, like not getting into university. Scales, such as the *social readjustment rating scale* (SRRS) have been developed that seek to

Additional studies

- Kanner et al. (1981) found by studying 100 participants aged 45–64 years over a 12-month period that, although the effects of uplifts was unclear, daily hassles correlated with undesirable psychological symptoms and were a better predictor of illness than life events. This suggests that daily hassles do contribute to stress-related illness.

- Rahe et al. (1970) assessed the number of life changes in sailors for the previous 6 months. Individual health records were scrutinised for a subsequent 6-month tour of duty, a positive correlation being found between LCUs and illness scores, suggesting a link between life changes and illness.

- Li Ping Tang & Hammontree (1992) found a link between occupational stress levels and absenteeism in police officers, again suggesting an association between life stress and illness.

- Sher (2004) found that heightened cortisol levels were associated with daily hassles in healthy individuals. As prolonged cortisol production is related to immunosuppression and daily hassles are continuous, it suggests that daily hassles lead to stress-related disorders.

Positive evaluation

✔ A practical application of research into life changes and daily hassles is that knowledge gained can help to form effective therapies to counteract the negative effects of such stressors.

✔ Instead of assessing if life changes or daily hassles contribute most to stress-related illness, it is better to focus on the mediating effect they have on each other. For example, life events can lead to daily hassles that result in physical illness, such as a person experiencing divorce, which leads to increased daily hassles in the form of increased housework, handling finances and so on.

objectively measure the relationship between life changes and stress-related illness. Although life changes have big impacts, they are only occasional; indeed most stress comes from the cumulative effects of the irritations and annoyances of daily hassles that build up as individuals go about their day. Daily hassles can create an elevated, continual level of stress that incurs a serious risk to health, although daily life can also incur *uplifts*, positive experiences that help to decrease stress levels. Attempts have also been made to measure daily hassles and uplifts, such as Kanner *et al.*'s (1981) hassles and uplifts scales.

▲ **Figure 4.3** Thomas Holmes was motivated to study stress-related illness after noting that he developed a cold every time his mother-in-law came to stay

Negative evaluation

✘ Many studies are retrospective and reliant on full and accurate memories. Davison et al. (2004) found that people's recollections of illnesses were different to what actually occurred. Therefore, only prospective studies that assess life events prior to the onset of illness are credible.

✘ The SRRS scale has predetermined scores for all life events. However, individuals experience events in dissimilar ways. The sudden death of a loved one is devastating for some, but the death of a loved one who has been suffering for a long time is a welcome release for others.

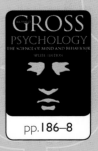

GROSS
PSYCHOLOGY
THE SCIENCE OF MIND AND BEHAVIOUR
SIXTH EDITION

pp.186–8

WORKPLACE STRESS

Focal study

Johansson et al. (1978) used Swedish sawmill workers to assess the influence of varying degrees of work responsibility and job repetitiveness as stressors affecting health. A high-risk group of ten finishers, whose jobs involved repetitiveness and high levels of responsibility, were compared with a low-risk group of ten cleaners. Stress was measured by the level of stress hormones in urine samples on work and rest days, health records and absenteeism levels. It was found that the high-risk group had higher levels of stress hormones than the low-risk group and higher levels on work days than rest days. The high-risk group also had more stress-related illnesses and more days absent from work. It was concluded that the workplace stressors of repetitiveness and high degrees of responsibility have a continual negative physiological effect on individuals that can lead to stress-related illnesses and absenteeism.

Description

The workplace can be a stressful environment and thus can have serious consequences for health, as well as having an impact on job performance through increases in accidents and absenteeism, and decreases in productivity and high staff turnover. Workplace stressors, aspects of the work environment that negatively impact on health, can *directly* affect health and job performance, as well as having an *indirect* effect through the development of unhealthy lifestyle practices like heavy drinking. Such stressors not only negatively impact on the health of individuals, but also incur heavy costs for employers and the health service. The Confederation of British Industry estimated

Additional studies

- Marmot et al. (1997) found employees with low job control three times likelier to have heart attacks than those with high job control, suggesting that low job control negatively impacts on health.

- Kivimaki et al. (2006) conducted a meta-analysis of 14 studies, finding that high job demand correlated with vulnerability to developing coronary heart disease, illustrating how workplace stressors negatively affect health.

- Russek (1962) found medical professionals performing high-stress jobs likelier to develop

cardiovascular diseases than individuals in low-stress jobs, suggesting a link between stress and heart disease, although there is no indication if it is a direct or an indirect link.

- Hobson & Beach (2000) found that managerial staff's hours of work were not directly related to psychological health, but correlated with individual perceptions of work stressors, which in turn were related to measures of psychological health. This implies that perceived workload is a better determinant of psychological health than actual workload, suggesting a cognitive element to stress-related health risks.

Positive evaluation

✔ Although the workplace can be a source of stressors that negatively impact on health, it is also a source of opportunities to elevate self-esteem, confidence and motivational levels and helps give individuals a feeling of purpose and fulfilment, all of which contribute to positive physical and psychological well-being.

✔ Research into workplace stressors has led to practical applications that lower stress levels and improve productivity. The Wedgwood pottery company introduced quality circles into Britain, where workers are given time off to suggest and discuss ideas to improve the workplace, giving workers a sense of job ownership, which helps reduce stress levels.

that the cost of absenteeism to industry was £19.9 billion in 2009. Non-stressed workers are much more productive and content, and therefore research in this area tries to identify important factors, so that effective strategies can be devised to reduce the impact of workplace stressors on individuals and society as a whole. The major workplace stressors that have been identified and researched include *workload, predictability and controllability of work role, environmental factors* and *ambiguity*. Individuals with low job control have been identified as more stressed, while contradictory results have been found regarding how stressful high workloads are.

Negative evaluation

✘ Findings and conclusions drawn from research into workplace stressors may quickly be redundant, as the workplace is an ever-changing environment, with the constant emergence of new forms of stressors to contend with — for instance, the introduction of new technologies, changing job practices and lower job security.

✘ Research into workplace stressors does not consider the impact of individual differences; stressors affect people in different ways and subsequent research has concentrated on assessing how personality is related to the experience of stress — for example, those high in hardiness cope better with stress.

▲ **Figure 4.4** The workplace contains many potential sources of stress

PERSONALITY FACTORS

Description

Research has indicated that individual differences in the way individuals perceive and react to stressors are related to personality factors. In studying the association between personality and stress, researchers have referred to *personality types*, general characterisations, where people share the same traits. Research focused on Type A Behaviour Pattern (TABP), originally suggested by Friedman & Rosenman (1959) when investigating non-physiological factors involved in coronary heart disease (CHD). TABP is characterised by *time urgency, excessive competitiveness* and *hostility,* and correlates with greater vulnerability to CHD and high blood pressure. Recent research suggests that hostility, characterised by non-specific dislike of others, the tendency to see the

Additional studies

- Davison & Neale (1994) reported that although studies showed Type A personality types were at greater risk of developing CHD and high blood pressure, the risks are only relative, as most Type As do not develop these disorders, while some Type Bs do.
- Greer & Morris (1975) found that females with breast cancer displayed more emotional suppression than those with non-life-threatening breast cancer, implying a link between Type C personality and cancer.
- Morris et al. (1981) found that Type C women suppress their emotions when stressed and are more vulnerable to developing cancer, due to emotional suppression leading to a weakening of the immune system and an increased risk of cancer.
- Kobasa (1979) proposed the hardy personality type, characterised by individuals having *control* over their lives, being *committed* to what they are doing and perceiving stressors as enjoyable *challenges*. Such personality traits resulted in diminished physical arousal when confronted by stressors and thus a reduction in stress-related illnesses, suggesting hardiness to be healthy.

Positive evaluation

✔ It may be considered unethical to perform research on Type C women suffering from cancer, as the additional stress of being studied could further negatively impact on health. However, through such research a greater understanding might be reached, leading to the formation of effective strategies that lessen the chances of Type C women developing cancer.

✔ Research suggests that the components comprising hardiness, namely control, commitment and challenge, are learnable, and therefore teaching individuals to develop these components helps to form an effective stress-management technique that lowers the risk of developing stress-related disorders.

worst in others, anger, envy and a lack of compassion, is the best predictor of CHD. Type B is a healthy personality type characterised by non-competitiveness, self-confidence and relaxation, and is not associated with stress-related illness. Type C relates to vulnerability to cancer, with individuals having difficulties expressing emotions and tending to suppress or inhibit negative emotions, displaying instead 'pathological niceness', conflict avoidance and overcompliance. Type D personality is characterised by distress, gloom, worry and lack of sociability, incurring risks of heart attacks, while hardiness is characterised by control, commitment and self-improvement and is associated with low vulnerability to stress-related disorders.

Negative evaluation

✘ There is no convincing evidence to suggest that people divide easily into separate personality types. Many individuals have personality characteristics that straddle several of the suggested personality types and there is a risk that in labelling people as a certain type, a self-fulfilling prophecy may occur, where people adopt the characteristics of the personality type they are deemed to have.

✘ Friedman & Rosenman did not control all aspects of lifestyle in their study of Type A personality and therefore it could well be that it is other factors that incur vulnerability to heart disease.

▲ **Figure 4.5** Type C women who are caring and helpful to others have an increased risk of cancer

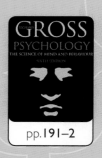

GROSS
PSYCHOLOGY
THE SCIENCE OF MIND AND BEHAVIOUR
SIXTH EDITION

pp.191–2

PSYCHOLOGICAL METHODS OF STRESS MANAGEMENT (SM)

Jay & Elliot (1990) assessed the use of SIT with parents of children suffering from leukaemia who were about to undergo stressful bone marrow treatment and lumbar punctures. The researchers created an SIT video film, and 1 hour before each child's treatment the parents were shown the film, which depicted a model parent employing coping self-statements, relaxation efforts and coping imagery rehearsal. Parents were then given an opportunity to practise these skills. The findings showed that in comparison to parents who received a child-focused intervention, the SIT-treated parents displayed less anxiety and superior coping skills. It was concluded that SIT is an effective treatment for acute, short-term stressors.

Description

Psychological SM techniques identify and address underlying causes of stress by focusing on how people manage perceptions of stress. *Cognitive behavioural therapy* (CBT) sees stress-related illnesses as resulting from irrational, maladaptive thoughts and tries to replace these with rational, adaptive thought processes. One form of CBT is *stress inoculation therapy* (SIT), which is applied before stress-related disorders develop. SIT involves cognitive restructuring that focuses on altering emotional responses and behaviour. The cognitive component involves recognition of stress symptoms, while the behavioural component involves using skills that act on causes of stress. The basic idea is that individuals can become resistant to stressors by previously being exposed to small doses of such stressors. SIT has three phases.

Additional studies

- Holcomb (1986) found that psychiatric patients responded better to SIT than drug treatments in reducing symptoms of anxiety, distress and depression. A 3-year follow-up study found that SIT-treated patients required fewer hospital admissions for psychiatric episodes, suggesting that SIT is superior in long-term treatment of stress disorders.

- Sarafino (1990) found that participants who underwent hardiness training developed lower blood pressure and felt less stressed than a control group who did not receive hardiness training, which suggests that hardiness is effective in addressing stress-related disorders. This was supported by Kobasa & Maddi (1977), finding that male white-collar workers who had undergone hardiness training also coped better with stressors.

- Dominiquez & Mestas (2002) reported that the introduction of hardiness training at Utah Valley State College had allowed students to master the stressors they encountered while studying, thus helping them to stay in and graduate from college, demonstrating the effectiveness of the technique in real-life settings.

Positive evaluation

✔ SIT is doubly effective, as it not only treats current stressors, but also inoculates against future stressors, because it has a long-term effectiveness and can used with many differing stressful incidents. Patients merely have to continue practising and applying the learned skills to stressful situations they encounter.

✔ Both SIT and hardiness training are based on solid theoretical foundations of a cognitive and behaviourist nature and both have research backing from laboratory and real-life backgrounds, giving the treatments solid support as effective, psychological SM techniques.

1. *Assessment*, where current strategies for dealing with stress are discussed.

2. *Stress-reduction techniques*, where skills are taught to deal with stress, like 'preparation techniques', which act as positive coping statements.

3. *Application and follow-through*, where patients visualise using learned SM techniques, then use them in role play and finally in real life.

Hardiness training is founded on Kobasa's (1986) idea of the hardy personality, which is seen as beneficial in resisting stress, and has three components.

a) *Focusing*, where individuals learn to realise when physical symptoms of stress need addressing.

b) *Reconstruction of stress situations*, where previous stressful incidents are revisited to understand current stressors and coping strategies.

c) *Self-improvement*, where individuals perceive stressors as challenges to be controlled.

Negative evaluation

✘ SIT can be problematic in that patients need to be motivated and committed over lengthy time periods, often difficult for those suffering from stress-related disorders to achieve, which suggests the treatment is not without its drawbacks.

✘ There are so many different components to SIT, such as relaxation, cognitive appraisal, life skills, that it is difficult to assess which are the most effective ones. Research has tended to indicate that relaxation may be the key factor.

✘ Hardiness may actually not exist. Funk (1992) stated that low hardiness scores merely indicate that people have negative thinking in relation to stressors and it is this that leads to negative health consequences.

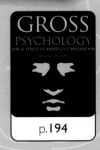

GROSS
PSYCHOLOGY
THE SCIENCE OF MIND AND BEHAVIOUR

p.194

BIOLOGICAL METHODS OF STRESS MANAGEMENT (SM)

Focal study

Sansone et al. (2003) investigated the relationship between BZ usage and the amount and degree of stressful trauma experienced. Fifty-three participants being treated with BZs for trauma, aged between 20 and 82 years, recorded their lifetime consumption of BZs and the length of time they were taken. Participants also completed a questionnaire assessing exposure to traumatic events, like traffic accidents, recording levels of fear, helplessness and horror. A positive correlation was found between the amount of BZ drugs taken and the number of different traumatic experiences. Positive correlations were also found between the number of traumatic experiences and the amount of BZ drugs taken, and the number of traumatic experiences associated with fear, helplessness and horror and the amount of BZ drugs taken. It was concluded that the degree of BZ usage is related to the amount of and degree of trauma experienced and that the cognitive characteristics of BZs help protect against re-experiencing traumas that were emotionally intense.

Description

Biological SM methods focus on physiological stress–response systems, where physical symptoms are perceived as causal factors, rather than mere effects. Drug therapies introduce chemicals into the bloodstream that affect *neurotransmitters*, chemicals aiding communication between brain nerve cells. Anti-anxiety drugs slow central nervous system activity, suppressing physical symptoms of anxiety. They are sometimes used as an initial treatment, with psychological treatments added on when symptoms lessen enough for such therapies to be effective. *Benzodiazepines* (BZs), like Valium, increase the effect of the neurotransmitter GABA, which has a dampening effect on brain neurons. GABA production

Additional studies

- Davidson (1993) found BZ drug treatment for social anxiety disorder more effective, 78% of participants improving, than placebo treatment, where only 20% improved. A two-year follow-up found better functioning in drug-treated participants than placebo-treated ones, indicating that BZ treatment is effective long-term.
- Zandstra et al. (2004) found it was older, less well-educated, lonely patients who used avoidant coping strategies when faced with stress, who took BZs for longer than the recommended time period. This suggests such patients should receive alternative treatments.
- Lau et al. (1992) found from a meta-analysis that BBs reduced risk of death by 20% in heart attack patients by lowering high blood pressure, suggesting that BBs are an effective treatment for such patients.
- Lindholm et al. (2005) found that the risk of strokes was 16% higher with BBs than other anti-hypertension drugs, but that treatment with BBs was superior to no treatment, suggesting that BBs are effective, but that there are better alternatives.

Positive evaluation

Positive evaluation

✔ BZs and BBs are easy to take, cost-effective and popular with patients, as they are a known and trusted form of treatment.

✔ BBs incur an immediate therapeutic effect, acting directly on the body to lower blood pressure and heart rate, and as such are highly recommended for use in cases of potentially fatal stress-related hypertension.

✔ BBs, unlike BZs, are not associated with risk of addiction and dependency and can be regarded as superior in this sense, though they can incur side effects like tiredness and hallucinations.

permits an increase of chloride ions into neurons, making it difficult for other neurotransmitters to stimulate them, leading to a slowdown in neural activity and a sensation of relaxation. BZs also dampen down the excitatory effect of serotonin, further slowing the nervous system and contributing to the feeling of calm. *Beta blockers* (BBs) block the transmission of nerve impulses, by 'sitting' on beta-adrenergic receptors, minute structures on cells that increase the force and rate of the heartbeat and stimulate adrenaline production, which during stress increases the heartbeat. Therefore BBs dampen the physical effects of stress by lowering the force and rate of the heartbeat.

Negative evaluation

✗ BBs are not effective as a long-term treatment for stress conditions with a psychological element, which suggests that their usage is limited to short-term treatment of physical symptoms.

✗ BBs and BZs do not address causes of disorders; such medications only temporarily halt negative stress effects. When treatment ends, symptoms may reappear.

✗ BZs are addictive, with withdrawal symptoms occurring when treatment stops, therefore treatment is recommended for a maximum of four weeks, but many people take them for longer, incurring addiction risks.

✗ BZs also incur serious side effects in some patients, like sexual dysfunction. This reduces their effectiveness, as such patients may stop taking them before achieving symptom reduction.

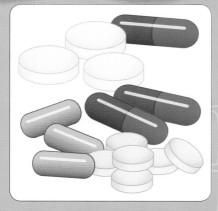

▲ **Figure 4.6** Drug treatments are a direct means of treating stress-related illness

TYPES OF CONFORMITY

Focal study

Asch (1955) investigated whether individuals would conform to an obviously wrong answer. 123 American volunteer male students were tested in groups of between eight and ten, with only one real participant who either answered last or next to last, the other group members all being confederates. Participants sat in a line or around a table, having been told that it was a study into visual perception. A stimulus line was presented with three comparison lines, one clearly matching the stimulus line while the other two did not. Participants had to say out loud which comparison line matched the stimulus. From 18 trials, confederates gave identical wrong answers on 12 occasions. There was a 32% overall conformity rate, 75% conforming at least once, 25% never conforming, while 5% conformed all the time. It was also found that most participants conformed publicly, but not privately, a form of *compliance*, in order to avoid rejection.

Description

Conformity occurs when a majority influences the beliefs and/or behaviour of a minority. There are three types, differing in terms of how much they affect individuals' belief systems.

1. *Compliance* involves public, but not private agreement with a group's beliefs and behaviour, in order to gain acceptance or avoid disapproval. It is fairly temporary and weak, only occurring within the presence of the group. For example, an individual professes allegiance to the local football team in order to fit in and be accepted, while in reality having little if any allegiance to the team.

Additional studies

- Sherif (1935) used the autokinetic effect, a visual illusion, to find that participants' second individual estimates of how far a dot of light in a dark room appeared to move converged towards a group norm after participants heard the estimates of others. This suggests that participants internalised others' judgements and made them their own.

- Crutchfield (1954) got participants to conform to obviously wrong answers, obtaining a similar conformity level to Asch, but with participants answering privately. This suggests that they complied for reasons other than a fear of ridicule, such as genuinely doubting the validity of their initial judgement.

- Bogdonoff et al. (1961) measured the stress levels encountered by participants on an Asch-type task, by recording galvanic skin responses, a measurement of electrical conductivity. High stress levels were found when participants gave true answers that went against the majority, but lower levels when individuals complied with obviously wrong answers, implying that compliance is the healthy thing to do.

Positive evaluation

✓ Asch's procedure became established as the accepted method of assessing conformist behaviour and as such is known as a **paradigm** study.

✓ The experimental set-up of Asch's study allowed him to vary parts of the procedure, such as having one confederate who went against the others by giving false answers, in order to identify the reasons for conformist behaviour.

✓ Mann (1969) believed internalisation to be **true conformity**, as it is the only type of majority influence where participants are actually converted to other people's belief systems.

2. *Identification* involves public and private agreement with a group's beliefs and behaviour because membership of that group is beneficial. A stronger type than compliance, it is still fairly temporary and weak, as it is not retained when an individual leaves the group. For instance, a soldier who, while in the army, adopts the beliefs and behaviour of fellow soldiers, then adopts new beliefs and behaviour on returning to civilian life.

3. *Internalisation* involves public and private agreement and is not dependent on group membership. For instance, beliefs in a religious faith are not dependent on group members being present, so this is the strongest form of conformity.

Negative evaluation

✗ There are other reported reasons for why people conform in Asch's study, such as having doubts about individual perceptual ability and the accuracy of individual judgements. Therefore it may not just be compliance that is occurring.

✗ Most studies of types of conformity, such as Asch, Crutchfield and Sherif, are unethical and could not be performed now, as they involve deceit and therefore a lack of informed consent, as well as causing distress through elevating stress levels.

✗ Asch's study was time-consuming, with only one participant being tested at a time. As 123 participants performed 18 trials each, the experiment was conducted 2,214 times.

▲ **Figure 5.1** Internalisation, such as through religious conversion, is a very strong type of conformity that does not require the presence of the group

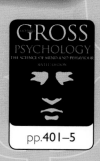

GROSS
PSYCHOLOGY
THE SCIENCE OF MIND AND BEHAVIOUR
SIXTH EDITION

pp.401–5

EXPLANATIONS OF CONFORMITY

Focal study

Insko et al. (1983) tested participants in groups of six, one of whom was a real participant, judging which of two coloured slides matched another. On critical trials confederates gave wrong answers. In one version participants answered privately or publicly to see if conformity was higher when participants answered publicly due to NSI, while in a second version the researcher either stated that he could or could not 'determine' which of the two options was most correct to see if conformity was higher in the 'determined' condition due to ISI. Both predictions came true and the 'determined' condition produced greater conformity in both public and private conditions, all four conditions producing greater conformity than a control condition with participants tested alone. It was concluded that even with 'objective stimuli', ISI can add to the effect of NSI, which suggests that the two explanations can operate together.

Description

Deutsch & Gerard (1954) suggested two explanations of conformity, *informational social influence* (ISI) and *normative social influence* (NSI). Underlying ISI is a need for certainty that brings a sense of control. ISI occurs in ambiguous situations with no clear 'correct' way of behaving, as well as novel situations not experienced before. In such situations, individuals look to the majority for information on how to behave. This therefore involves *social comparison* with others in order to reduce uncertainty – for instance, when voting in an election for the first time and asking others who they are voting for because you have not enough political experience to make up your own

Additional studies

- Jenness (1932) got participants to estimate the number of jellybeans in a jar, first as individuals, then in groups and finally individually again, finding that participants' second individual estimates moved towards the group norm. As this was an uncertain situation, individuals looked to others for information on how to behave through ISI.

- Asch (1955) performed a variation of his paradigm study where he made all the comparison lines similar to each other, finding that participants became increasingly likely to conform to the wrong answer. As the task was now uncertain, it suggests that the explanation for the conformist behaviour changed from NSI to ISI.

- Bond & Smith (1996) conducted a meta-analysis of Asch-type studies conducted across different cultures and at different times in one culture, finding that conformity declined over time in the USA and that independent cultures had lower levels of conformity than collectivist ones, suggesting that explanations of conformity differ over time and across cultures.

Positive evaluation

✔ Asch initially criticised Jenness's earlier study as inferior due to having no obvious wrong answer to conform to. However, both studies are equally effective in helping to highlight explanations for conformity; namely ISI in Jenness's case and NSI in Asch's case.

✔ As well as having research support, both NSI and ISI can be used to explain and understand real-life examples of conformist behaviour, giving them additional support as explanations.

✔ NSI explains the amount of negative and positive attitudes to groups as being related to how socially acceptable such groups are.

mind. ISI therefore involves stronger types of conformity, such as internalisation, where public and private agreement with a majority occurs. Underlying NSI is a need to belong, by being accepted and avoiding rejection and ridicule. Therefore individuals agree with others, because of their power to reward and punish – for instance, giving in to peer pressure to smoke, even though it may go against your true wishes, in order to be accepted by the group. NSI therefore tends to involve a weaker form of conformity and compliance, where public, but not private agreement occurs.

Negative evaluation

✗ It is difficult to separate out NSI from ISI. For instance, although Asch's study mainly involves NSI where participants know their answers are incorrect, some participants did conform for informational purposes, as they did not trust their perceptual judgements. In Jenness's study, participants conformed due mainly to ISI, but there was also an element of people conforming to avoid ridicule, which suggests that NSI was also occurring.

✗ Although they aid understanding of conformist behaviour, explanations of conformity can sometimes have negative connotations, like how NSI can lead to destructive inter-group violence.

▲ **Figure 5.2** ISI occurs where individuals look to others for how to behave, such as to ascertain correct etiquette in a restaurant

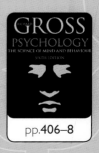

pp.406–8

THE WORK OF STANLEY MILGRAM

Milgram (1963) tested 40 volunteer American males, aged between 20 and 50 years, on their willingness to obey increasingly destructive orders. Believing it to be a study of memory and learning, they draw lots with a second participant, actually a confederate, to see who will be the 'teacher' and the 'learner'. This was rigged; the real participant is always the teacher. The learner is strapped into a chair in an adjacent room with electrodes attached to him. It is explained by a confederate researcher, who wears a laboratory coat to give him legitimate authority, that every time the learner gets a question wrong the teacher must shock him by pressing a switch on a (fake) shock machine. If the teacher refuses, the researcher orders him to carry on with a series of verbal 'prods'. The shocks went up in 15-volt increments to 450 volts, which is administered three times. Initially happy to comply, the learner begins to protest and at 300 volts refuses to continue. At 315 volts he screams loudly and is not heard from again. 100% of participants obeyed up to 300 volts and 62.5% went to 450 volts, even though some wept, argued and three had seizures. It was concluded that obeying authority figures is usual in a hierarchically arranged society, even when orders violate our moral codes.

Description

Obedience is defined as *'complying with the demands of an authority figure'*. Milgram, from a working-class New York Jewish family that had fled Europe before the Holocaust, was interested in understanding how 10 million Jews and Gypsies were exterminated on the orders of the Nazis during the Holocaust. He set out to test the 'Germans are different' hypothesis, which argued that the Holocaust occurred because Germans

Additional studies

- Burger (2009) developed an ethically acceptable variation of Milgram's study, with participants explicitly given the right to withdraw. Using males and females, an obedience rate of 70% was found, suggesting that Milgram's study can be conducted ethically and that obedience rates have not changed in the nearly 50 years since Milgram's study.
- Sheridan & King (1972) assessed the claim that Milgram's participants obeyed as they knew the procedure was false, by using a puppy who received real electric shocks. Out of 26 participants, 20 complied to the end, including all 13 female participants, which suggests that Milgram's results were valid and that females are even more obedient.
- Hofling et al. (1966) assessed the claim that such obedience would not occur in the real world, getting a pretend doctor to order real nurses to give an apparent overdose to a patient. Out of 22, 21 obeyed, suggesting that obedience to destructive orders from a legitimate authority does occur in the real world.

Positive evaluation

✔ A valuable insight was gained into obedient behaviour, which can be used to teach people to recognise and resist attempts to get them to comply with immoral orders. 74% of Milgram's participants said they had learned something useful about themselves and only 2% regretted being involved.

✔ Milgram's is a paradigm study, the accepted method of researching obedience, which allowed comparison of obedience rates in different countries, between genders, ages and occupations.

blindly obey authority figures. Milgram showed that people are more obedient than they realise, getting participants to carry out apparently painful acts against an unobjectionable stranger purely because a researcher ordered them to. Many objected to the researchers' commands, but obeyed them to the end, showing that individuals do not necessarily agree with orders that they obediently carry out.

Negative evaluation

✘ Milgram's study is criticised as unethical for the following reasons:

1. It involves deceit through the use of confederates being told the shocks were real and that the study was one of learning and memory.

2. A lack of informed consent, as deceit was used.

3. No right of withdrawal.

4. Psychological harm. Milgram argued that because they could withdraw, as 37.5% of them did, the harm was only short-term, was reduced by debriefing and made justifiable by the valuable findings.

✘ Orne & Holland (1968) believed that the study lacked internal validity, arguing that participants knew the shocks were fake; however, 80% stated they had 'no doubts' about the authenticity of the study.

▲ **Figure 5.3** Stanley Milgram

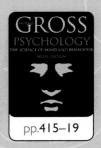

GROSS
PSYCHOLOGY
THE SCIENCE OF MIND AND BEHAVIOUR
SIXTH EDITION

pp.415–19

EXPLANATIONS OF OBEDIENCE

Milgram (1974) performed a series of variations to identify reasons for obedience:

1. *The learner was silent throughout* – 100% obedience, as proximity to the consequences of the behaviour was low.

2. *Study performed in a run-down office block* – 48% obedience, as the perception of legitimate authority was reduced, increasing personal responsibility.

3. *Victim in same room as the teacher* – 40% obedience, as increased proximity to the consequences of the behaviour was increased.

4. *Teacher forces learner's hand onto a shock-plate* – 30% obedience, as increased proximity to the consequences of the behaviour was increased.

5. *Experimenter not present, but phones orders in* – 20.5%, as the agentic state was reduced, increasing personal responsibility.

6. *Teacher is paired with two confederates who disobey* – 10% obedience, as the agentic state was reduced, increasing personal responsibility.

7. *Teacher reads out questions, but does not give shocks* – 92.5% obedience, as personal responsibility is decreased.

Description

From Milgram's studies, a number of explanations of obedience were identified.

1. *Perception of legitimate authority*, where participants obey as they accept the status and power of the researcher, making it hard to disobey.

2. *The agentic state* – where participants see themselves as *agents* of the authority figure, thus giving up and transferring personal responsibility onto the researcher.

3. *Personal responsibility* – where anything detracting from the status of authority figures increases the participants' sense of responsibility for their actions (known as the *autonomous state*, the opposite to the agentic state).

Additional studies

- Hamilton (1978) found, in a replication of Milgram's study, that when participants were told they were responsible for what happened, obedience reduced, suggesting that an increase in personal responsibility and the autonomous state leads to a reduction in obedience.

- Meeus & Raajimakers (1986) replicated Milgram's study, finding an obedience rate of 92% in a Dutch sample, while Kilham & Mann (1974) found an obedience rate of 40% in Australian males and 16% in Australian females, suggesting that obedience rates vary across genders and cultures, implying that different explanations are needed for each.

- Tarnow (2000) found that a major contributory factor to 80% of aeroplane accidents was co-pilots feeling that they could not challenge wrong decisions by the captain, due to the perceived power and legitimacy of his authority, suggesting that the perception of legitimate authority helps to explain obedient behaviour.

- Bickman (1974) found that participants obeyed orders from someone dressed in a uniform more than someone dressed as a milkman or in smart casual clothes, again suggesting that perceived legitimate authority explains obedience.

Positive evaluation

✔ Bickman's study is valuable, because as a field experiment it occurred in a real-life setting and is high in **ecological validity**; indeed participants did not even know they were in a study, which implies that their actions were not artificial.

✔ Milgram's variations turn each study into an experiment (something the original study is not) as they create independent variables through comparison with the findings from his standard procedure. For example, when the learner is in the same room as the teacher, it creates an IV of whether the learner was visually present or not.

4. *Entrapment*, where Milgram's participants were gradually drawn into obeying. Initial demands were mild, such as volunteering for a study, then giving mild shocks to someone agreeable to it, before becoming progressively destructive, by which time participants found it increasingly harder to disobey destructive orders.

5. *Dehumanisation*, where the recipient of the harmful behaviour, the 'learner' was belittled as being *'so stupid he deserved to get shocked'*.

6. *Proximity*, where the closer participants were to the consequences of their behaviour, the less obedient they were.

7. A further explanation of obedience is *socialisation*, where obedient behaviour is 'ingrained' into individuals from an early age by powerful socialising agents, such as parents and teachers.

Negative evaluation

✘ Smith & Bond (1998) believe it is not really possible to compare Milgram-type obedience studies conducted in different cultures and across genders and so on, as often methodologies differed. For instance, Kilham & Mann (1974) used a long-haired male learner, while Meeus & Raajimakers (1986) got participants to harass someone completing an application form, which may have created a dehumanising effect.

✘ It can be difficult to assess which explanation is applicable to an act of obedience; indeed several factors may be at play at once.

▲ **Figure 5.4** Obedience can be explained by the perception of legitimate authority, such as through uniforms

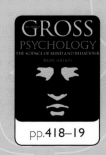

GROSS
PSYCHOLOGY
THE SCIENCE OF MIND AND BEHAVIOUR
SIXTH EDITION

pp.418–19

LOCUS OF CONTROL

Avtgis (1998) conducted a meta-analytic review of studies involving LoC and conformity, where the average effect size for internal and external locus of control was measured. Earlier research had indicated that those scoring high on external LoC are more easily persuadable, socially influenced and conformist than those who score high on internal LoC. After subjecting the data to statistical analysis, it was found that these predictions were generally true, with participants who displayed an external locus of control being more easily persuadable and more likely to conform. These results support the idea that differences in conformist behaviour are related to differences in measures of LoC, although this is only a correlation and therefore does not show causality, as other factors may be involved too.

Description

Rotter (1976) identified *locus of control* (LoC) as a personality dimension. LoC relates to the extent to which individuals see themselves as having control. People who believe they can influence the outcomes of situations have *high internal LoC*, while those who believe that they cannot influence the outcomes of situations have *high external LoC*. The idea that events occur, due to personal choices and decisions relates to *internal LoC*, while *external LoC* relates to the idea that events occur due to luck, fate or other external, uncontrollable factors. An internal LoC makes individuals more resistant to social pressure, those who believe they are in control of outcomes being likelier to perceive themselves as having a free choice to conform or obey.

Additional studies

- Twenge *et al.* (2004) found that more Americans are developing external LoC, as a result of increased mental illness, suicide and divorce. This suggests that Americans have become less independent in their behaviour and thus are less able to resist conformity and obedience.

- Shute (1975) found that students with internal LoC conformed less to expressing pro-drug attitudes, which suggests that having an internal LoC increases an individual's ability to resist conformity.

- Moghaddam (1998) found that Japanese participants had higher levels of external LoC and conformed more than Americans, which implies that differences across cultures in conformity levels is explicable by reference to LoC.

- Jones & Kavanagh (1996) found that participants with high external LoC were likelier to obey unethical orders from authority figures, suggesting that those with high LoC are more able to disengage from the moral consequences of their actions.

When individuals experience success/failure they make *causal attributions*, attempting to understand why things happen the way they do. From these, individuals develop *attributional styles* that they apply to future events, so that attitudes and behaviour become predetermined. Independent behaviour is where individuals are resistant to conformity and obedience is displayed by those with a *positive explanatory style*, where others are blamed for failure and failure is seen as temporary. Non-independent behaviour, with individuals likelier to conform and obey, is shown by those with a *depressed attributional style*, where they believe themselves incapable of turning failure into success and being unable to influence events.

Positive evaluation

✔ Reference to different types of LoC and the extent to which people are affected by social influences, such as conformity and obedience, gives us an understanding of the role that personality plays in conformist and obedient behaviour, and demonstrates that situational factors alone cannot explain such behaviours.

✔ Chiu (2004) believes that the rise in corporate fraud, where large financial corporations embezzle billions of pounds, is understandable by reference to junior staff having external LoC that allows them to comply with illegal orders given to them by senior staff. Conversely, 'whistle-blowers', people who report such irregularities at the risk of losing their jobs, have high internal LoC.

Negative evaluation

✘ The general scales of measurement, like the Rotter scale, on which LoC is assessed, may not be suitable for investigating independent behaviour in specific situations.

✘ It is simplistic to perceive conformity and obedience as caused by internal and external LoC, as it is likelier that behaviour in given situations is dependent on whether external or internal factors dominate.

✘ Attribution theory sees external (situational) factors as leading to conformist and obedient behaviour and internal (personality) factors as leading to independent behaviour. However, there are situational factors related to independent behaviour and personality factors linked with conformist and obedient behaviour.

RESISTING CONFORMITY AND OBEDIENCE

Richardson (2009) assigned 84 male and female participants to same-sex groups of three, where two of each group were confederates and one a naive participant. The naive participants were told they were newcomers to the groups and all members were to introduce themselves. The confederates always went first and either described themselves as high-status or low-status in terms of education, experience and so on. The groups then had to decide which of two stock companies to invest in, one being evidently superior to the other. The confederates answered first and selected the weaker of the two options. It was found that in the teams where confederates claimed to be high status, participants conformed to the majority decision, while in the teams where confederates claimed to be low status, conformity was lower. It was concluded that status does affect conformity and that competence-based clues are used to determine levels of conformist behaviour.

Description

Studies of conformity and obedience provide insight into how conformity and obedience can be resisted. In a variation of Asch's study, if a *dissenter* disagreed with the majority, then conformity dropped, even if the dissenter was not agreeing with the real participant. This shows how dissenters give individuals social support to resist majority influence. *Reactance*, rebellious anger, also leads to independent behaviour – for instance, young people often rebel against conforming to adults' rules. Yet another means to independent behaviour is that of *ironic deviance*, where if individuals believe that a source of informational influence is not

Additional studies

- Hamilton et al. (2005) found that adolescents in a low-reactance group who were told it was normal to try drugs, as long as they knew the health risks, were less likely to smoke than those in a high-reactance group told never to smoke. This supports the idea of reactance being linked to independent behaviour.
- Conway & Schaller (2005) found that individual office workers conformed to using a software product on the recommendation of co-workers, but were less likely to do so if they believed the co-workers were ordered to recommend it. This suggests

ironic deviance, where sources of information are distrusted, which increases independent behaviour.

- Martin et al. (2007) found that if participants were encouraged to consider the content of unreasonable orders, they were less likely to obey, demonstrating how systematic processing increases resistance.
- Kohlberg (1969) found that participants from Milgram's study who based decisions on moral judgements were less obedient, supporting the idea that morality is linked to independent behaviour.

Positive evaluation

✔ The knowledge gained from studies involving resistance to obedience can be used in the training of staff, especially those working in institutions like hospitals, so that they are encouraged to follow official procedures, not authority figures, and to challenge potentially harmful orders.

✔ It is clear from research that has been carried out that to avoid people complying with destructive orders, time should be taken to consider the potential consequences of obedience, and that people should make reference to internal personal moral codes before making a decision about whether to comply or not.

real, conformity to that influence will be resisted. *Status* also affects conformist behaviour, as those with higher status are more likely to resist. *Systematic processing* is a means by which obedience can be resisted. This involves individuals having time to consider whether they feel orders are unreasonable or not. *Morality* is also linked to resisting obedience, in that individuals who consider the consequences of obeying orders in terms of their personal moral beliefs are more likely to resist immoral orders. *Personality factors* can also affect obedience and conformity, with arguments being put forward for the existence of conformist and obedient personality types.

Negative evaluation

✘ The idea that people divide up into separate personality types is simplistic. Adorno (1950) proposed an authoritarian personality, where individuals who are rigid and inflexible, prejudiced to minorities and servile to authority figures, obey readily, with those possessing opposite traits seen as resistant. Similar claims are made for conformist/non-conformist personality types, but actually most people do not divide up so easily into set personality types.

✘ Not all examples of non-conformist behaviour are true examples of resistance to conformity. Often people will move away from majority group expectations, but towards the expectations of a minority group.

▲ **Figure 5.5** People of high morality are more resistant to destructive obedience

UNDERSTANDING SOCIAL CHANGE AND THE ROLE OF MINORITY INFLUENCE IN SOCIAL CHANGE

Description

Social change can be beneficial, like increased rights for homosexuals, but can also be destructive, like the resulting genocide from the Nazi regime. While majority influence is a force requiring little thought, helping maintain things the way they are, minority influence is a form of social influence, requiring consideration, which leads to social change. Thus social change occurs slowly, but gradually, as minority viewpoints build up until they become majority viewpoints, changing people's attitudes and beliefs over time. This type of conformity is strong and long-lasting and is a form of internalisation, as it involves conversion of belief systems. In this way,

Additional studies

- Meyers et al. (2000) found that minority groups successful in influencing majorities were more consistent than those who were not, supporting Moscovici's findings.
- Nemeth & Kwan (1987) found that tasks requiring divergent thought (thinking simultaneously in different ways) were performed better with minority influence. However, Petersen & Nemeth (1996) found that tasks requiring convergent thought (focusing on one aspect) were performed better with majority influence, implying that it is the nature of a task that determines whether

minority influence is best and leads to social change.

- Martin & Hewstone (1996) found that more novel and creative outcomes resulted from minority than majority influence, supporting the idea of minority influence being a source of innovation and social change.
- Martin et al. (2003) found messages supported by minority groups more resistant to persuasion than with majority groups, suggesting that cognitive processing of minority opinions leads to attitudes resistant to counter-persuasion, illustrating the strength of minority influence that leads to social change.

Positive evaluation

✔ Minority influence works best when it occurs privately, whereby the converted majority does not have to publicly abandon the majority position.

✔ Minority influence gives us a means of comprehending how innovative social change occurs, allowing beneficial changes to occur, in a gradual, evolved manner that has undergone a lot of considered reasoning. In this way, social change occurs that benefits society and allows us to meet new challenges and utilise modern technologies in a positive, constructive manner.

innovation occurs, permitting new, radical ideas and behaviours to be accepted and become mainstream practices. For example, Greenpeace, the environmental campaign group, began in Canada in the early 1970s and initially was a minority viewpoint, ridiculed for its 'crackpot' ideas. Gradually people converted to their viewpoint, slowly at first, but more quickly as the group gained increased support, a process known as *social cryptoamnesia* (the snowball effect). Eventually Greenpeace became the mainstream, accepted voice for environmental issues. For minorities to be influential they need to be *consistent, flexible, committed* and *relevant*.

Negative evaluation

✘ There is more to minority influence than just consistency. Nemeth et al. (1974), on a Moscovici-type task, found no minority influence with consistency, but found it was important how the majority interprets the minority's answers, which must relate to a stimulus in some predictable way to be influential.

✘ Clark & Maas (1990) found no minority influence effect on a majority group larger than four people, which suggests that minority influence is restricted in its ability to convert and incur social change.

✘ Moscovici's study only used females and thus his findings may not be generalisable to males, especially as many studies have found females to be more conformist than males.

▲ **Figure 5.6** Minority group behaviours, which initially may be scorned and rejected, can over time be a source of innovation and social change that results in them becoming mainstream activities. For example, jogging was considered bizarre in the 1970s but is now a widespread, and completely normal activity

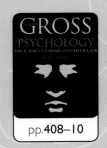

GROSS
PSYCHOLOGY
THE SCIENCE OF MIND AND BEHAVIOUR
SIXTH EDITION

pp.408–10

THE DEVIATION FROM SOCIAL NORMS DEFINITION OF ABNORMALITY

Limitation

✗ Social norms are not real in an objective sense, but are subjective, being based on the opinions of a society's elite, and are then used to police those seen as challenging the social order.

Limitation

✗ Social norms actually refer to moral standards that change over time, like homosexuality once being classed as a mental disorder. A truly objective definition would not have such variations.

Limitation

✗ Those who deviate from social norms may simply be individualistic or eccentric, rather than abnormal.

Description

The deviation from social norms definition of abnormality implies that there is a 'correct' and 'incorrect' way of behaving and that any deviation from the 'correct' way is abnormal. The social norms that there is an expectation for individuals to adhere to are therefore a set of unwritten rules of what is acceptable behaviour that have been constructed by society. There is an argument that these norms are set by the ruling elite within a society and are more a means of policing people and maintaining social order than an objective definition of what is normal and abnormal. The deviation from social norms definition permits a distinction between what is seen as desirable and undesirable behaviour, classifying those exhibiting undesirable behaviour as *socially deviant*. This gives society through its controlling institutions, like the health service, the right to intervene in people's lives in order to protect the rest of society and to 'treat' social deviants so that they can become 'normal' again and be returned to mainstream society. The definition can be seen as beneficial to abnormal individuals,

Limitation

✗ Szasz (1962) argued that the definition is used to justify discriminating against sections of society as a form of social control, with some countries, such as China, categorising political opponents as being abnormal and then forcibly treating them in mental institutions.

Limitation

✗ There are individuals who adhere so strictly to social norms that they can be considered conforming neurotics, a form of abnormality where such individuals fear rejection and ridicule so much that they conform rigidly to society's norms and worry excessively about them, yet such individuals are not classified as abnormal by the deviation from social norms definition.

▲ **Figure 6.1** Having a tantrum is considered normal for a 2-year-old, but not for older ages

as deviants, such as those classed as sexually deviant, may be unable to recognise that their behaviour is maladaptive and therefore unable to seek help by themselves. The deviation from social norms definition can also be seen to have a social dimension to the concept of abnormality, as it perceives the main purpose of mental health care as being to exclude individuals from society who are seen as behaving in unacceptable ways. There are several types of social norms to which adherence is expected:

1. *Situational/contextual norms*, where certain behaviours are expected/not expected in certain situations. For example, it is acceptable for females to wear a bikini on the beach, but not in a supermarket.

2. *Developmental/age norms*, where certain behaviours are expected at different times in one's lifespan. For example, temper tantrums are perfectly normal for a 2-year-old to exhibit, but not for a 40-year-old.

3. *Cultural norms*, where certain behaviours are acceptable/unacceptable in different cultural settings, like homosexuality being accepted in Western cultures, but not in African ones.

Limitation

✗ The definition can be seen to have an ethnocentric bias, where cultural norms reflect the behaviour of the dominant group within a culture, and minority ethnic groupings are judged on these norms to such an extent that they become overrepresented in those classed as abnormal. Sharpley et al. (2001) reported that black British people are more often classed as schizophrenic than white people. However, there is no such overrepresentation of black people in countries where they are the majority. This suggests a cultural bias in diagnosis by British psychiatrists, the vast majority of whom are white.

Limitation

✗ Sometimes for society to experience positive social change it is necessary to break social norms. This can be seen as a form of minority influence, where the majority deride and perceive minority views that violate social norms, before coming round to accepting the minority view as a new form of social norm. For example, the campaigning of suffragettes broke social norms to achieve better rights for women in society.

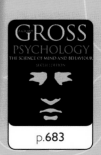

GROSS
PSYCHOLOGY
THE SCIENCE OF MIND AND BEHAVIOUR
SIXTH EDITION

p.683

THE FAILURE TO FUNCTION ADEQUATELY DEFINITION OF ABNORMALITY

Limitation

✗ Mental disorders are not always accompanied by personal dysfunction; indeed the opposite may be true. Harold Shipman, a Lancashire doctor with a psychopathic antisocial personality disorder, displayed an outwardly normal disposition, while over a 23-year period as a doctor, murdering at least 215 of his patients before killing himself in prison.

Limitation

✗ What is perceived as 'normal functioning' in one culture may be perceived completely differently in another culture. This means that perceptions of normal functioning are subjective and should not be used as a standard to judge people from other cultures by.

Limitation

✗ Some of the features comprising 'adequate functioning' are subjective themselves and difficult to define and measure objectively. This also applies to individual differences between people. What is normal behaviour for introverts, like wearing non-flamboyant clothes, would be completely different for extroverts and the definition fails to incorporate this.

Description

The failure to function adequately definition of abnormality sees mental disorders as resulting from an inability to cope with day-to-day living. Behaviour is perceived as abnormal when individuals become so distressed with the pressures of everyday life that behaviour becomes dysfunctional – for example, when an individual's ability to work properly is compromised, or when individuals cannot conduct normal interpersonal relationships. Due to an inability to cope with life, harmful behaviours are indulged in, like heavy drinking or drug taking, which in themselves are dysfunctional, but also contribute to further deterioration in personal functioning, leading to a diagnosis of abnormality. Rosenhan & Seligman (1989) proposed that personal dysfunction has seven features and that the more of these features an individual has, the more they are classed as abnormal:

1. *Personal distress*, which is seen as a key feature of abnormality and involves such manifestations as depression and anxiety disorders.

2. *Maladaptive behaviour*, which consists of exhibiting behaviour that prevents people from realising their life goals, both socially and occupationally.

▲ **Figure 6.2** Most people with mental disorders seek clinical help themselves for their problems

Limitation

✗ Although an individual's behaviour may be distressing to others and perceived as an inability to function adequately, it may bring no distress to the individual and be perceived by them as perfectly functional. For example, Stephen Gough is known as the 'naked rambler' for his long-distance walks that he conducts in the nude. He has been jailed many times for his behaviour, which he sees as perfectly normal and causes him no distress.

3. *Unpredictability*, which consists of exhibiting unexpected behaviours characterised by a loss of control, like mutilating oneself after a relationship is terminated.

4. *Irrationality*, which consists of exhibiting behaviours non-explicable in any rational way, like heavy drinking in response to work pressures.

5. *Observer discomfort*, which entails the exhibition of behaviours that cause discomfort to others, like behaving in an aggressively provocative manner.

6. *Violation of moral standards*, which consists of exhibiting behaviours that contravene society's ethical standards, like being naked in a public place.

7. *Unconventionality*, which entails the exhibition of non-standard behaviours, like dressing in the clothes of the opposite gender.

The failure to function adequately definition is supported by the fact that the vast majority of people seeking clinical intervention do so because they perceive that they have mental difficulties that interfere with their ability to function properly, both socially and occupationally. Overall, this is a definition that focuses on individuals' perceptions of their own mental health and is simple to judge objectively, through criteria such as 'can hold down a job', 'is able to dress themself' and so on.

Limitation

✗ Experiencing distress and not being able to function adequately are things that are totally normal in response to some common life events, and indeed not to be distressed by such events and being able to function adequately would be considered abnormal. For example, it is expected and even psychologically healthy to feel distress and an inability to function normally in response to the death of a loved one.

Limitation

✗ Some behaviours that seem to reflect distress and an inability to function adequately, and which are thus perceived as abnormal, may in fact be totally adaptive and functional for an individual. For example, some individuals who wear the clothes of the opposite gender do it for occupational reasons and earn a sizeable amount of money for doing so.

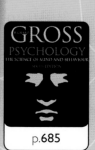

GROSS
PSYCHOLOGY
THE SCIENCE OF MIND AND BEHAVIOUR
SIXTH EDITION

p.685

THE DEVIATION FROM IDEAL MENTAL HEALTH DEFINITION OF ABNORMALITY

Limitation

✗ According to these criteria, most people, if not all, would be abnormal most of the time. Therefore the criteria are over-demanding — for example, few people experience continual personal growth, indeed the opposite may be periodically common. Self-actualisation is seen as something that very few people achieve — so does this mean the majority of us are abnormal? The criteria may actually be ideals of mental health, how we would like to be, rather than how we actually are.

Limitation

✗ Many of the criteria are subjective, being vague in description and rather hard to measure in any objective way. Measuring physical indicators of health is generally easy — for example, by using blood tests and scans — but diagnosis of mental health is much trickier and relies largely on the self-reports of patients, who, if they have a mental disorder, may not be reliable.

Limitation

✗ As with other definitions, many of the criteria of the deviation from mental health definition are affected by context/situation. Spitting while out running is regarded as quite acceptable, but not so when in the college cafeteria.

Description

The deviation from ideal mental health definition of abnormality concentrates on identifying the characteristics and abilities that people should possess in order to be considered normal. Therefore a lack of or impoverishment of these characteristics and abilities constitutes a diagnosis of abnormality. The definition therefore has a perception of mental disorders as being similar to that of physical health, in that an absence of well-being means that an individual is ill. Jahoda (1958) devised the concept of ideal mental health and identified a set characteristics that individuals need to exhibit to be seen as normal. The more of these criteria an individual fails to realise and the further away they are from meeting individual criteria, the more abnormal they are considered to be. Similarly to the deviation from social norms definition and the failure to function adequately definition, the deviation from ideal mental health definition also concentrates on behaviours and characteristics that are seen as desirable, rather than undesirable. A positive aspect to this definition is that it stresses positive accomplishments rather than failures and distress. There are six characteristics of ideal mental health:

Limitation

✗ Autonomy, seen as desirable by the definition, is a Western cultural ideal. Collectivist cultures stress communal goals and behaviour and thus regard autonomy negatively and as undesirable. Nobles (1976) argues that Africans tend to have a sense of 'we' that differs from the more selfish European sense of 'me', with people from Western cultures being more concerned with individual achievements and goals.

1. *Positive attitude towards oneself*, which involves having self-respect and a positive self-concept, where individuals regard themselves favourably.

2. *Self-actualisation*, where individuals should experience personal growth and development. Self-actualisation involves 'becoming everything one is capable of becoming'.

3. *Autonomy*, which concerns individuals being independent, self-reliant and able to make personal decisions.

4. *Resistance to stress*, where individuals should be in possession of effective coping strategies in response to stress and should be able to cope with everyday anxiety-provoking situations.

5. *Accurate perception of reality*, where individuals should be able to perceive the world in a non-distorted manner and possess an objective and realistic perception of the world.

6. *Environmental mastery*, which concerns individuals being skilled in all aspects of their lives, both socially and occupationally, and being able to meet the requirements of all situations they experience. Additionally, individuals should possess the flexibility to be able to adapt to changing life circumstances, again, both socially and occupationally.

Limitation

✗ The characteristics used to assess mental health are culturally relative and should not be used to judge people from other cultures and subcultures. For instance, some mental disorders only exist in certain cultures, such as koro, found only in South East Asia, China and Africa, which is a disorder concerning the belief that a man's penis is fatally retracting into his body. Therefore Western cultural views of abnormality, like the deviation from ideal mental health definition, are equally not culture-free.

Limitation

✗ What is perceived as 'reality' changes over time. Seeing visions was once regarded as a religious talent, but would now be diagnosed as a marker of schizophrenia.

▲ **Figure 6.3** Jahoda's criteria may be more to do with ideal than actual mental health

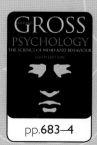

GROSS
PSYCHOLOGY
THE SCIENCE OF MIND AND BEHAVIOUR
SIXTH EDITION

pp.683–4

THE BIOLOGICAL APPROACH TO PSYCHOPATHOLOGY

Focal study

Hideyo & Moore (1913) assessed the relationship between the syphilis bacterium and the neuropsychiatric disorder **general paralysis of the insane** (paresis). Post-mortem examinations were performed on 70 individuals aged between 33 and 60 years who had died from paresis in the Central Islip State hospital, with brain tissue samples being silver stained to reveal the bacterium. Syphilis bacterium was found in ten males and two females, which suggested that infection with syphilis is necessary for the later development of paresis and that therefore brain infections can cause mental illness in line with the biological approach. Patients in whom syphilis bacterium were found tended to be individuals where the disease had developed rapidly, and thus the bacterium may have been easier to find in such patients. The bacterium may not have been found in some, as the disease was confused with other similar diseases, especially in its final stages.

Description

The biological approach is the main method by which abnormal conditions are understood, with medical terminology used to describe their features. The approach perceives mental disorders as having physiological causes related to the physical structure and functioning of the brain, to be *diagnosed*, *treated* and *cured*, as with physical illnesses. The model has two categories: *organic* disorders, involving brain damage and disease, and *functional disorders*, with no discernible physical cause, like depression. As with physical disorders, clinicians use diagnostic criteria to classify mental disorders as being identifiable, separate syndromes, each described in terms of symptoms. In Britain, clinicians use the *International Classification of Diseases, 10th edition* (ICD-10), while American psychiatrists use the *Diagnostic and Statistical Manual of Mental Disorders,*

Additional studies

- Sousa et al. (2010) compared the DNA of 1,000 autistic individuals to 1,200 non-autistic individuals, finding that autistic individuals had 20% more *copy number variations*, genetic material that distinguishes people from each other and affects brain development. This suggests a genetic link to autism.

- Zubieta et al. (2000), using PET scans, found that people with manic depression had 30% higher levels of the monoamine brain chemicals dopamine, serotonin and norepinephrine, which implies that disruption of biochemistry can lead to mental illness.

- Tien et al. (1990) found that heavy and persistent abuse of cocaine and/or amphetamines can result in brain damage, which in turn leads to psychosis, illustrating how brain damage can cause mental illness.

- Brown et al. (2000) reported an association between respiratory infections in the second trimester of pregnancy and the foetus subsequently developing schizophrenia on reaching adulthood. This suggests that bacterial infections and viruses can cause mental illness.

Positive evaluation

✔ The biological model is a humane approach, as patients are not seen as responsible for their actions, in the same way as someone contracting a cold is not responsible for sneezing.

✔ The biological approach has paved the way for the development of effective treatments, like the antipsychotic drugs that have greatly improved the lives of many people with schizophrenia. The fact that certain disorders respond favourably to therapies based on the biological approach can also be seen as supporting evidence for the model.

✔ The biological approach is founded on well-established scientific principles that allow testing by objective experimental methods, permitting replication to check results.

4th edition (DSM-IV). There are four ways in which biological factors are linked with mental abnormalities:

1. *Bacterial infections and viruses* – for instance, *general paralysis of the insane*, a neuropsychiatric disorder caused by syphilis.

2. *Brain damage*, through disease or accident, like the memory loss associated with *Alzheimer's disease* through destruction of nerve cells.

3. *Biochemistry*, through disruption of hormone and neurotransmitter levels, like elevated dopamine levels in schizophrenics.

4. *Genetic factors*, like the linking of autism to hereditary factors.

Negative evaluation

✘ Szasz (1962) argues that mental illness is a myth. The mind does not exist in any physical sense, so cannot be diseased like the body can. He also argues that a diagnosis of mental illness is a method of 'social controlling' of undesirable elements of society.

✘ Concordance rates between biological factors and mental disorders are never 100%, which they would be if biological factors were solely responsible for abnormalities. The diathesis-stress model proposes that people have genetically determined degrees of vulnerability to mental disorders, but that disorders only develop in the presence of certain amounts of environmental stressors.

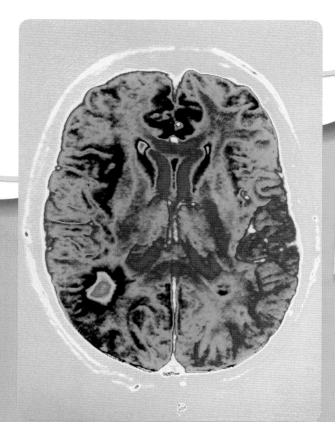

▲ **Figure 6.4** Brain damage through disease is associated with some mental disorders

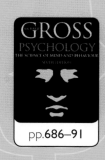

GROSS
PSYCHOLOGY
THE SCIENCE OF MIND AND BEHAVIOUR
SIXTH EDITION

pp.686–91

THE PSYCHODYNAMIC APPROACH TO PSYCHOPATHOLOGY

Focal study

Freud (1909) reported on the case study of a 5-year-old child, Little Hans, conducted through correspondence with his father. Hans developed a phobia of horses after seeing one fall over in the street, and also endured attacks of general anxiety to such an extent that he was afraid to leave the house. Freud interpreted Hans's phobia of horses as representing a *castration complex*. This fitted into Freud's idea of the *Oedipus complex*, where during the phallic stage boys develop intense sexual love for their mothers and a fear that their more powerful fathers will punish them through castration. A coping mechanism was seen as developing, namely '*identification with the aggressor*', where Hans came to identify with his father, adopting his attitudes, beliefs and behaviour to resolve his fears. At age 19 Hans confirmed that he had experienced a happy adolescence and was fit and well.

Description

The psychodynamic approach is a psychological model associated with Freud. The model sees mental disorders as developing from unresolved, unconscious childhood traumas. Freud saw personality consisting of three parts:

1. The *id*, present at birth and governed by the *pleasure principle* to seek immediate gratification.

2. The *ego*, which develops through experience at age 2, based on the *reality principle*.

3. The *super-ego*, which develops around age 5 to 6, consisting of the moral beliefs making up one's conscience, governed by the *morality principle*.

Additional studies

- Williams (1994) found from interviews that 38% of 129 women sexually abused during childhood could not recall the abuse, which had been reported 17 years earlier, especially those abused by someone they knew. This supports Freud's idea that traumatic events occurring during development through the psychosexual stages are repressed into the unconscious mind.

- Massie & Szajnberg (2002) performed a longitudinal study up to age 30 on 76 participants' childhood parental relationships and also recorded details of traumatic events, to find a positive correlation between poor-quality parental relationships and traumatic events experienced during childhood, thus lending support to Freud's theory.

- Ito (1998) used PET scans to find that the id is located in the limbic system, while the ego and super-ego are located elsewhere in the frontal lobes of the cerebral cortex. This was supported by the similar findings of Solms (2000), which supports the existence of the id, ego and super-ego and suggests that they have a physiological basis.

Positive evaluation

✔ The model is important, being the first to perceive mental disorders as psychologically based, inspiring lots of interest and research into the origins of abnormality that has furthered our understanding of mental conditions.

✔ The model has inspired the creation of therapies, namely psychoanalysis, which many see as having improved the quality of their lives and assisted them to come to terms with mental disorders, especially those linked to traumatic events in childhood. Most psychologists agree that unconscious processes can affect behaviour.

Freud saw individuals as progressing through a series of *psychosexual stages:*

1. The *oral stage*, from 0 to 1 year, pleasure coming from sucking and chewing.

2. The *anal stage*, from 1 to 3 years, pleasure coming from evacuating the bowels.

3. The *phallic stage*, from 3 to 6 years, pleasure gained from the genitals.

4. The *latency stage*, from 6 to 12 years, with less concentration on sexual matters.

5. The *genital stage*, from adolescence onwards, pleasure gained from heterosexual relationships. Freud believed the ego faced a constant struggle to balance out the conflicting demands of the id and super-ego, and that unresolved traumas during the psychosexual stages were repressed into the unconscious mind, to emerge in adulthood as abnormalities.

▲ **Figure 6.5** Sigmund Freud

Negative evaluation

✗ The model over-stressed childhood influences at the expense of adult ones and over-stressed sexual factors, due to the sexually repressed age Freud lived in. Modern psychoanalytic theory recognises this and stresses the important role that inadequate interpersonal relationships and everyday problems play in developing abnormal conditions.

✗ The model lacks falsifiability and cannot be tested in a scientific manner. Scodel (1957) tested Freud's claim that over-mothered men preferred large-breasted women due to being more orally dependent, but found they preferred small-breasted women. This appears to refute the claim, but Freudians argue that the men are in denial of their preference, illustrating the non-testable nature of the theory.

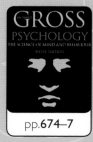

GROSS
PSYCHOLOGY
THE SCIENCE OF MIND AND BEHAVIOUR
SIXTH EDITION

pp.674–7

THE BEHAVIOURAL APPROACH TO PSYCHOPATHOLOGY

Focal study

Watson & Rayner (1920) assessed whether emotional responses are learned through classical conditioning, by performing a laboratory experiment on Albert, an 11-month-old boy. Albert was presented with various stimuli, including a white rat, a rabbit and some cotton wool, and his responses were filmed. He displayed no fear of any of the objects. A fear reaction (*unconditioned response*) was then induced by striking a steel bar behind Albert's head (*unconditioned stimulus*), which made him cry. He was given a white rat to play with (*conditioned stimulus*) and the steel bar was struck to frighten him. This was done three times and repeated over a three-month period. Subsequently when shown the rat, Albert cried and rolled away. He had developed a *conditioned response* of fear towards the rat, which generalised itself to other white furry objects. It was concluded that conditioned emotional responses occur as a direct result of environmental experience.

Description

The behaviourist model is a psychological approach that perceives mental disorders, indeed all behaviour, as being learned through the processes of *classical conditioning, operant conditioning* and *social learning*. The emphasis is on observable, measureable behaviour, rather than hidden mental processes, as with the psychodynamic and cognitive approaches. Behaviourism sees mental disorders as *maladaptive behaviours* and rejects the medical model's notion of separate syndromes (illnesses) distinguishable by symptoms. Classical conditioning is a form of learning that acts on reflex actions through a neutral stimulus acquiring the properties of non-neutral stimulus through association. For example, pho-

Additional studies

- Krafft-Ebing (1886) reported the case of a man who gained sexual pleasure through being punished, as a result of accidental friction on his penis while being spanked across an adult's lap as a child. This implies that his masochistic tendency was developed through classical conditioning where arousal became associated with physical punishment.
- Wikler (1973) reported that initiation of drug addiction occurs through classical conditioning, but that maintenance of drug dependency occurs via operant conditioning, where drug taking is negatively reinforced through the termination of withdrawal symptoms when taking drugs.
- Becker (1999) found that before television was introduced to Fiji in 1995, it was very rare for young women to be conscious of their weight, but by 1998, 74% thought they were too fat or big and eating disorders started to occur. This suggests that a social learning effect had occurred through observation and imitation of skinny role models in television programmes.

Positive evaluation

✔ The behaviourist approach is a very scientific one that permits objective, measurable experimentation and is able to produce explanations of some abnormal conditions that are backed up by solid research evidence.

✔ The model is advantageous, as it accounts for individual differences and social and cultural contexts by its perception that maladaptive behaviours are shaped by individual environmental experiences, often ones that are unique.

✔ The fact that the behavioural model focuses on present behaviour is also advantageous in revealing causes of disorders, as errors of recall and partial memory of events can occur by asking people about their past.

bias can be acquired by a neutral object or situation being paired with a fear response. Operant conditioning involves learning through *reinforcement*, where if a behaviour is rewarded, it strengthens the chances of it recurring. For instance, being rewarded through praise and attention for losing weight can increase dieting behaviour until anorexia nervosa is developed. Social learning theory sees abnormal behaviours being learned by *vicarious reinforcement*, where a role model is observed and imitated if their behaviour is seen as being reinforced. For example, imitating the drug-taking behaviour of one's peers, who attract admiration for their behaviour, could lead to drug dependency.

Negative evaluation

✗ Although the model presents a creditable explanation of how phobias are acquired, the approach cannot explain naturally occurring phobias, which are more explicable by reference to evolutionary theory. Many Irish people have snake phobias, but there are no snakes in Ireland to have negative experiences with.

✗ Behaviourism, by concentrating only on observable behaviour, is guilty of ignoring more important underlying causes.

✗ As the model over-stresses the role of environmental factors, at the expense of biological and internal psychological factors, behaviourism finds it difficult to explain disorders with no clear learning factors, such as schizophrenia.

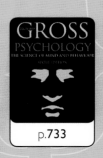

GROSS
PSYCHOLOGY
THE SCIENCE OF MIND AND BEHAVIOUR
SIXTH EDITION

p.733

▲ **Figure 6.6** Positive reinforcements can see dieting progress to anorexia

THE COGNITIVE APPROACH TO PSYCHOPATHOLOGY

Description

The cognitive approach concentrates on thinking, focusing on the mental processes occurring between stimuli and responses, as it is these that relate to how individuals feel about stimuli. There is an overlap with the behaviourist approach, as there is acknowledgement of the role that maladaptive learning plays, but with the addition of maladaptive thought processes. Mental disorders occur due to distorted and irrational thought processes, like negative thoughts and illogical beliefs, referred to as *cognitive errors*. These influence emotions and behaviour, leading to abnormalities. *Automatic thoughts* occur without deliberate efforts and individuals with mental disorders have more of them.

Additional studies

- Gustafson (1992) found that individuals suffering from depression, sexual problems and anxiety disorders displayed signs of maladaptive thinking, supporting the cognitive approach.
- Abela & D'Alessandro (2002) found that students identified as at risk of depression due to maladaptive attitudes who did not get into their university of choice, doubted their scholastic abilities and developed depression. This implies a cognitive cause to depression through maladaptive thought processes.
- Clark (1986) reported that panic attacks resulted from catastrophic misinterpretation of bodily sensations associated with anxiety responses, like breathlessness and dizziness. These responses were misinterpreted as more dangerous than they were, such as perceiving palpitations as a heart attack, which suggests that maladaptive thought processes are related to certain mental disorders.
- Armfield (2007) assessed spider phobias, finding that those who believed they could not remove themselves from a spider's presence, those told a spider was dangerous and those told its movements were unpredictable, scored highly on fear of spiders, demonstrating that personal beliefs determine levels of cognitive vulnerability, supporting the model.

Attributions involve attempts to make sense of one's own and others' behaviour, and people with mental disorders make more of these too – for example, having inaccurate expectations that all relationships will end in failure. Such expectations may then occur through a *self-fulfilling prophecy*. Overall the approach sees abnormalities occurring when maladaptive thinking leads to maladaptive behaviour. For example, Beck (1963) saw depression occurring through the *cognitive triad* (three illogical thought processes), resulting in irrational feelings that lead to depression:

1. *Negative feelings about themselves* – for example, 'nobody loves me'.
2. *Negative feelings about the future,* – for example, 'I will always be useless'.
3. *Negative views about oneself,* – for example, 'I have no value'.

Negative evaluation

✘ Depression may not always result from maladaptive thought processes, but instead may be a logical reaction to negative life events.

✘ The model emphasises individual responsibility for maladaptive thinking, but this neglects the important role that situational factors, like negative life events, and biological factors, such as genetics, play in determining mental disorders.

✘ Thought processes cannot be directly observed or measured, which makes the approach difficult to test in an objective, scientific manner.

✘ It is not clear whether maladaptive thought processes are the cause or effect of mental disorders.

▲ **Figure 6.7** People with irrational negative thoughts are more vulnerable to developing depression

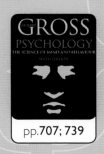

pp.707; 739

BIOLOGICAL THERAPIES

Description

Drugs enter the bloodstream to reach the brain and affect transmission of neurotransmitters, which then modify behaviour. *Antagonists* block the effects of neurotransmitters, while *agonists* mimic or increase effects. There are six main types:

1. *Antimanics*, which treat manic and severe depression by calming over-stimulated brain areas.

2. *Antidepressants*, used against depression by increasing serotonin production.

3. *Anxiolytics*, which treat stress and phobias by calming central nervous system activity.

4. *Antipsychotics*, which lower dopamine activity in schizophrenics.

5. *Stimulants*, which improve mood and alertness by triggering the release of noradrenaline and dopamine.

6. *Hypnotics*, which promote sleep.

Additional studies

- Gelder *et al.* (1999) reported that the main difference between different types of anti-depressants was their degree of side effects rather than their effectiveness, as they all increase serotonin production, with most also affecting dopamine production, and they all take about 10–14 days to 'kick in' and all should be withdrawn slowly, as sudden cessation causes insomnia, anxiety and nausea.

- Bergqvist *et al.* (1999) found that the antipsychotic drug risperidone reduced symptoms of OCD by lowering dopamine levels, suggesting the treatment is effective against the disorder.

- Benton (1981) reported that although bilateral ECT is more effective against severe depression, unilateral ECT has fewer side effects, which suggests that both treatments have strengths and weaknesses.

- Johnstone (1999) reported that some patients perceive ECT as a damaging repeat of earlier physical/sexual abuse, which suggests that assessment of patients should occur pre-treatment to identify those for whom ECT is not suitable.

- Tharyan & Adams (2005) found that ECT was an effective short-term treatment of schizophrenia, but not as effective as anti-psychotic drugs.

Electroconvulsive therapy (ECT) is used with drug-resistant depression and has been reintroduced as a treatment for schizophrenia. Treatment occurs several times a week for 6 to 12 treatments. A general anaesthetic and muscle relaxant are given, so that pain and fractures are not experienced. There are two types of ECT:

1. *Unilateral*, occurring through stimulation of the non-dominant hemisphere.

2. *Bilateral*, occurring through stimulation of both hemispheres. It is thought that ECT induces changes in neurotransmitter levels, increasing sensitivity to serotonin in the hypothalamus, and increases the release of GABA, and noradrenaline and dopamine levels.

Positive evaluation

✔ Drugs are comparatively cost-effective, easy and familiar to take and patients have confidence in them.

✔ There is a large body of clinical evidence suggesting drugs to be effective. Antipsychotics are effective for two-thirds of psychotic patients and 80% of schizophrenics.

✔ There is no evidence that ECT damages the brain. Coffey (1991) used MRI scans to report no signs of brain damage after ECT treatment.

✔ ECT is an effective treatment for severe depression and schizophrenia that have proven resistant to other treatments.

✔ Depressives who are non-responsive to other treatments are at high suicide risk. Therefore ECT is a lifesaver in such cases.

Negative evaluation

✘ Drugs have side effects. Atypical anti psychotics cause tremors, while some drugs are addictive, with other side effects including nausea, insomnia and damaged immune systems.

✘ ECT side effects are severer in children, adolescents, the elderly and pregnant women, suggesting that ECT should not be used with such patients, unless as a last resort.

✘ 84% of ECT patients relapse within 6 months, while 50% of schizophrenics responding favourably to treatment relapse inside six months, suggesting that ECT is not a long-term treatment.

▲ **Figure 6.8** ECT is used to combat depression, especially when other treatments have failed

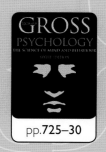

GROSS
PSYCHOLOGY
THE SCIENCE OF MIND AND BEHAVIOUR
SIXTH EDITION

pp.725–30

PSYCHOLOGICAL THERAPIES

Description

Psychological therapies offer alternatives to dominant biological therapies. No single psychological therapy is best; each has strengths and weaknesses and is effective with specific disorders.

Psychoanalysis is derived from the psychodynamic model, treatment requiring an analyst using various techniques to bring repressed traumas into the conscious arena to give insight into disorders.

Dream analysis involves interpretation of a dream's *manifest content* (what dreams appear to be about) as its *latent content* (their deeper meaning), while *free association* involves relaxing the 'internal censor' so that unconscious material appears symbolically for therapists to interpret.

Additional studies

Leichsenring (2001) reported that the success rate of short-term psychoanalytic treatments for depression was comparable to that of CBT. As CBT is highly regarded, this suggests that psychoanalysis is an effective treatment of depression.

Rachman & Wilson (1990) report that SD is most effective in treating specific phobias, such as animal phobias, which have developed through negative learning experiences, and for patients capable of learning relaxation skills and with sufficiently vivid imaginations to conjure up sources of their fear. This suggests that SD should be a treatment targeted at those who would benefit most from it.

Beck (1993) reviewed evidence to find that CBT was highly effective in treating against depression, generalised anxiety disorder, panic disorder and eating disorders, and was also effective in treating drug abuse, patients with cancer, HIV, OCD, PTSD and schizophrenia. This suggests that CBT has a broad application that bolsters the claims of cognitive therapy as being a robust form of treatment.

Positive evaluation

✓ Modern types of psychoanalysis occur over a shorter time-span and focus more on current than past events, producing swifter improvements, and are more cost-effective.

✓ SD is relatively quick to administer and requires less input from patients than other therapies.

✓ SD can be modified successfully for use with different types of people with different requirements, like adolescents and the elderly, which emphasises its wide-ranging application.

✓ CBT occurs over a relatively short time period in comparison to other treatments and is more cost-effective than other treatments.

Systematic desensitisation (SD) is a behaviourist therapy that replaces maladaptive behaviours with adaptive ones by using classical conditioning to replace irrational fears associated with phobic objects/events with relaxation responses, as the two opposite emotions of fear and relaxation cannot exist simultaneously. Patients use muscle relaxation in response to being exposed to phobic objects/situations in scenarios of rising intensity. *Cognitive behavioural therapy* (CBT) is based on the cognitive approach and challenges and restructures maladaptive thought processes into adaptive ones. Maladaptive thoughts produce negative self-statements, so CBT aims to replace these with rational, positive ones by patients being taught to recognise negative automatic self-statements and by practising optimistic thinking.

Negative evaluation

✗ Classic psychoanalysis requires clients to attend three to five therapy sessions a week for several years, and this, for many, is too expensive, as well as being too time-consuming. This suggests that it is not a cost-effective treatment.

✗ SD is mainly applicable to treating anxiety disorders and as such is ineffective against the majority of mental disorders.

✗ CBT is difficult to assess. Different measurement scales are used by different researchers, which produce radically different rates of improvement.

✗ CBT is dependent on patients being able to think and talk rationally and therefore is not suitable for treating severe mental disorders such as schizophrenia.

GROSS
PSYCHOLOGY
THE SCIENCE OF MIND AND BEHAVIOUR
SIXTH EDITION

pp.730–2;
734–75

▲ **Figure 6.9** SD has been used successfully to treat fear of technology

MAKING THE MOST OF EXAMINATIONS

The exams

For the AS qualification, students sit two papers:
1. Unit 1 is divided into two sections: first, the cognitive psychology topic of *memory*, and second, the developmental psychology topic of *attachment*. Research methods questions are incorporated into both these sections, focusing on memory and attachment issues. Unit 1 comprises 50% of the total AS marks, with 72 marks on offer: 24 marks for memory, 24 marks for attachment and 24 marks for research methods.
2. Unit 2 is divided into three sections: first, the biological psychology topic of *stress*, second, the social psychology topic of *social influences*, and third, the individual differences topic of *abnormality*. Unit 2 comprises 50% of the total AS marks, with 72 marks on offer: 24 marks for stress, 24 marks for social influences and 24 marks for abnormality. All questions on both unit papers must be answered.

Examination injunctions

Exam questions use examination injunctions, the type of words used in questions to inform students what kind of answers are required. An understanding of these terms allows you to confidently write exam answers that match the requirements of the questions and thus gain access to all the marks on offer.
AO1 – *Identify* means simply to name, no other description is required. *Define* involves explaining what is meant by. *Outline* means give brief details without explanation. *Describe* means give a detailed account without explanation. *Correctly complete* means to fill in the missing information. *Select* means to choose the correct option.
AO2 – *Give* means to show awareness of. *Explain* means to give a clear account of why and how something is so. *Evaluate* means to assess the value or effectiveness of. *Discuss* means to give a reasoned, balanced account (including descriptive material). *Apply* means to explain how something can be used.

Types of exam questions

Exam questions are only asked about topics listed on the specification, with questions occurring in varying formats requiring certain types of answers.

- **Selection questions** involve pieces of information that candidates select and put into the correct parts of a table. There will be one spare piece of information so that a choice always has to be made.

- **Short-answer questions** are worth a few marks, exactly how many is stated in brackets after the question, giving some indication of how much material is be supplied to get full marks. Such questions could require description of knowledge, such as *'Outline two workplace stressors (4 marks)'*, or require evaluation, such as *'Explain one strength of the working memory model (2 marks)'*.

- **Stem questions** provide candidates with a scenario containing information drawn from topic areas outlined on the specification. To answer such questions, candidates refer to information contained within the scenario to illustrate their knowledge of the topic area and their ability to evaluate that knowledge. For example, *'Elidh has money problems, a situation that has been going on for some time and from which she cannot see any escape. She has problems sleeping, cannot concentrate at work and feels continually run down. With reference to the scenario, explain the effects of stress on Elidh (6 marks)'*.

- **Research methods questions** will occur on the Unit 1 paper and will centre on both memory and attachment topics, concentrating specifically on methodological issues, including ethical concerns. For example, *'a) Explain one strength of the strange situation testing procedure (2 marks); b) Outline one ethical issue concerned with the procedure (2 marks)'*.

- **Long-answer questions** require students to write a mini-essay. There will be one of these questions on the Unit 1 paper and one on the Unit 2 paper, which can occur on any of the topic areas outlined on the specification. These questions will be worth 12 marks, 6 of which will be for description of knowledge and 6 of which will be for evaluation. For example, *'Outline and evaluate the multi-store model of memory (12 marks)'*.

▲ **Figure 7.1**

PREPARING FOR EXAMINATIONS

How to revise exam questions

When first practising exam questions you will need all learning materials to hand, like notes and hand outs. Ensure you fully understand the requirements of the question from the command words and know how much to write by reference to the number of marks on offer. Make a plan in numbered bullet point form, and then have a go at writing your answer, only giving yourself the same amount of time as in the real exam (about 1 minute and 15 seconds per mark). You will probably have to refer to learning materials when writing your answer, but as you become familiar with this method, you will increasingly be able to write answers without them. A good way to achieve this is to read through relevant materials first, then put them away before writing your answer.

Revision strategies

Many students incorrectly see revision as something done immediately before examinations. Although pre-examination revision is important, revision is something that should be incorporated into your studies throughout the course and indeed is an integral part of the learning process. At the end of studying each element of a topic, you should revise the material to develop a deeper understanding and to check that all material has been covered and is fully understood. The best way to achieve this is to engage with the material – for example, by reading through notes/worksheets and so on, highlighting the main points. Make use of available textbooks to further elaborate your knowledge; better candidates will be making use of more than just one source of information.

Making a revision timetable

Before commencing pre-exam revision, you will need a revision timetable. This is best achieved by having morning, afternoon and evening sessions for each day. You can then use this as a template for each separate week of revision. For each of your subjects, make a list of the topics you need to revise. Then, using a pencil at first, slot in the topics, making sure that you first block out any sessions that are not available due to other commitments. It is probably best to initially revise subjects and topics that will be examined first. A revision programme has to be achievable, so ensure that there are a few spare slots each week to use if any planned revision sessions do not occur. When you have finally got all the topics entered, colour them in using a different colour for each subject. Put your revision timetable up on a wall and tick off sessions as you go. You might even give a copy to a parent so they can police you and make sure sessions get done. Having a revision timetable like this increases confidence that revision can be completed, which in turn increases motivation to actually revise.

▲ Figure 7.2

After this, attempt an exam-type question to assess your level of knowledge and understanding, and also to familiarise yourself with the kind of questions you may ultimately be asked.

Such questions can be accessed on the AQA website by reference to previous exam questions and to sample questions. These also include advice on what types of things to include in your answer. Over time make sure that you include all types of possible questions in your revision, not just those concerning outlining and describing, but also those requiring explanations and evaluations.

Pre-examination revision

- All topics need to be revised, including ones you find difficult, as they have an equal chance of being on the exam paper.
- Ensure you have listed all the topics on the specification and have all materials necessary for revising each topic.
- Find somewhere comfortable to revise, away from distractions.
- Make sure that everything you need for revising, like tidying up your desk, is done before revision starts. It is easy to spend all the designated revision time on distraction activities, like sorting out books and sharpening pencils.
- About 90 minutes a session will be best, using the revision method you have practised all year, namely, reading through necessary materials, highlighting important points, using previous exam questions to construct answers.
- Give yourself a planned reward for completing revision sessions, be it chocolate or a favourite TV programme.
- Revising in a constant, organised way like this is the best route to maximising exam performance.